5th Edition

Series 63
Uniform Securities Agent State Law Exam

License Exam Manual

KAPLAN FINANCIAL EDUCATION

SERIES 63 UNIFORM SECURITIES AGENT STATE LAW EXAM LICENSE EXAM MANUAL, 5TH EDITION
©2012 Kaplan, Inc.

If you find imperfections or incorrect information in this product, please visit www.kfeducation.com and submit an errata report.

Published in March 2012 by Kaplan Financial Education.

Printed in the United States of America.

ISBN: 978-1-4277-4079-3 / 1-4277-4079-8

PPN: 3200-2568

Contents

1   Regulation of Persons   1

1.1   **Definitions Under the Uniform Securities Act   3**
The Uniform Securities Act of 1956 (USA) ■ Administrator ■ Blue-Sky Laws ■ Person ■ Broker/ Dealer ■ Agent ■ Investment Adviser ■ Investment Adviser Representative ■ Issuer ■ Nonissuer ■ Security ■ Exempt Security ■ Exempt Transaction ■ Guaranteed ■ Offer/Offer to Sell ■ Sale ■ Fraud ■ SRO ■ Solicitor ■ Accredited Investor ■ Registrant ■ Institution ■ National Securities Markets Improvements Act of 1996 (NSMIA) ■ State

1.2   **Broker/Dealers and Agents   8**
Broker/Dealer ■ Agent

1.3   **Investment Adviser   18**
SEC Release IA-1092 ■ Exclusions from the Definition of Investment Adviser ■ Exemption from Registration for Investment Advisers ■ Registration Requirements for an Investment Adviser

1.4   **Investment Adviser Representative   30**
Registration Requirements for Investment Adviser Representatives ■ Exclusions from the Definition of Investment Adviser Representative ■ Investment Adviser Representative Termination Procedures

1.5   **Summary of the Four Securities Professionals   32**

1.6   **General Registration Procedures   34**
Submitting an Application ■ Provide Consent to Service of Process ■ Payment of Initial and Renewal Filing Fees ■ Post-Registration Requirements ■ Effectiveness of Registration

2 Regulations of Securities and Issuers 49

2.1 What is a Security Under the Uniform Securities Act? 51
List of Securities Under the Uniform Securities Act ■ Nonexempt Security ■ Issuer

2.2 Registration of Securities Under the Uniform Securities Act 55
National Securities Markets Improvement Act of 1996 (NSMIA) ■ Methods of State Registration of Securities

2.3 Exemptions from Registration 60
Exempt Securities ■ Exempt Transactions ■ Administrator's Power Over Exemptions ■ Summary of Exemptions from Registration

2.4 State Securities Registration Procedures 66
Filing the Registration Statement ■ Filing Fee ■ Ongoing Reports ■ Escrow ■ Special Subscription Form ■ Prospectus Delivery Requirements

3 Remedies and Administrative Provisions 77

3.1 Authority of the Administrator 79
Offer or Offer to Sell and Sale or Sell ■ Legal Jurisdiction of the Administrator

3.2 Actions to be Taken by the Administrator 83
Rules, Orders, and Forms ■ Conduct Investigations and Issue Subpoenas ■ Issue Cease and Desist Orders ■ Deny, Suspend, Cancel, or Revoke Registrations ■ Nonpunitive Terminations of Registration

3.3 Penalties and Liabilities 90
Civil Liabilities ■ Criminal Penalties ■ Judicial Review of Orders (Appeal)

3.4 Other Provisions 95
Filing of Sales and Advertising Literature ■ Administrative Files and Opinions

4   Ethical Practices and Fiduciary Obligations   103

4.1   **Antifraud Provisions of the USA   105**
Fraudulent and Prohibited Practices

4.2   **Dishonest and Unethical Business Practices of Broker/ Dealers and Agents   109**
Delivery Delays ■ Churning ■ Unsuitable Recommendations ■ Unauthorized Transactions ■ Exercising Discretion ■ Margin Documents ■ Commingling of Customer and Firm Assets ■ Improper Hypothecation ■ Unreasonable Commissions or Markups ■ Timely Prospectus Delivery ■ Unreasonable Servicing Fees ■ Dishonoring Quotes ■ Market Manipulation ■ Guaranteeing Against Loss ■ Disseminating False Trading Information ■ Deceptive Advertising Practices ■ Failing to Disclose Conflicts of Interest ■ Withholding Shares of a Public Offering ■ Responding to Complaints ■ Front Running ■ Spreading Rumors ■ Backdating Records ■ Waivers ■ Investment Company Sales ■ Practices Relating Solely to Agents

4.3   **Unethical Business Practices of Investment Advisers   121**
Suitability of Recommendations ■ Discretionary Powers ■ Excessive Trading ■ Unauthorized Trading ■ Third Party Trading ■ Borrowing From Clients ■ Lending to Clients ■ Misrepresenting Qualifications ■ Third Party Reports or Recommendations ■ Unreasonable Advisory Fees ■ Conflicts of Interest ■ Guaranteeing Results ■ Advertising ■ Unauthorized Disclosures ■ Improper Custody ■ Written Requirement for Contracts

4.4   **Fiduciary Responsibilities When Providing Investment Advice   127**
Principal or Agency Transactions ■ Agency Cross Transactions ■ Uniform Prudent Investors Act of 1994 (UPIA)

4.5   **General Rules Applying to Investment Advisers   130**
Investment Advisory Contracts ■ Brochure Rule ■ Custody of Client Funds and Securities ■ Periodic Inspections of Investment Advisers

4.6   **Section 28(e) Safe Harbor   138**

4.7   **Using the Internet   141**

4.8   **Sales of Securities at Financial Institutions   142**
Setting ■ Customer Disclosure and Written Acknowledgment ■ Communications with the Public ■ SIPC Coverage

4.9   **Currency Transaction Reports (CTRS)   143**

Glossary 155

Index 161

Series 63 Introduction

INTRODUCTION

Thank you for choosing this exam preparation system for your educational needs and welcome to the Series 63 License Exam Manual. This manual has applied adult learning principles to give you the tools you'll need to pass your exam on the first attempt.

Some of these special features include:

- exam-focused questions and content to maximize exam preparation;
- an interactive design that integrates content with questions to increase retention; and
- integrated SecuritiesPro™ QBank exam preparation tools to sharpen test-taking skills.

Why Do I Need to Pass the Series 63 Exam?

State securities laws require most individuals to pass a qualification exam to sell securities within their states. Almost all states require individuals to pass the Series 63 exam as a condition of state registration.

Are There Any Prerequisites?

Although there are no prerequisites for Series 63, some states require you to pass a FINRA exam, which is a corequisite exam that must be completed in addition to the Series 63 before a individual can become registered with a state. You may take either exam first (we recommend taking the FINRA exam first) but must complete both satisfactorily before you are fully licensed.

What Is the Series 63 Exam Like?

The Uniform Securities Agent Law Examination consists of 65 multiple-choice questions. The questions are prepared by NASAA, the North American Securities Administrators Association. Applicants are allowed 75 minutes to complete the test. Of the 65 questions on the exam, 60 will count toward the final score. The remaining 5 questions are being tested for possible inclusion in the test bank for future use. These questions may appear anywhere in the exam and are not identified.

What Score Must I Achieve to Pass?

You need a score of at least 72% (43 of 60 correct) on the Series 63 exam to pass and become eligible for registration as a Securities Agent.

What Topics Will I See on the Exam?

As far as exam coverage is concerned, the official title of the exam tells the story. This is the *Uniform Securities Agents State Law Examination*. Almost every question will deal with some aspect of state securities laws and practices prohibited or required by those laws. There are virtually no questions about securities products, but you will need to know enough about them to understand their suitability for different clients.

The questions you will see on the Series 63 exam do not appear in any particular order. The computer is programmed to select a new, random set of questions from a very large test bank for each exam taker, selecting questions according to the preset topic weighting of the exam. Each Series 63 candidate will see the same number of questions on each topic, but a different mix of questions. The Series 63 exam is divided into two critical function areas:

	# of Questions	% of Exam
State Securities Acts and Related Rules and Regulations	36	60%
Ethical Practices and Fiduciary Obligations	24	40%

When you complete your exam, you will receive a printout that identifies your performance in each area.

TAKE NOTE   Although the exam is divided into only two broad categories, there are several sub-categories in the first broad topical area. That area is further subdivided as follows:

	# of Questions	% of Exam
Regulation of Persons (broker/dealers, agents, investment advisers, and investment adviser representatives)	24	40%
Regulations of Securities and Issuers	6	10%
Remedies and Administrative Provisions	6	10%

Ethical Practices and Fiduciary Obligations covers the broad range of proper behavior and deals with communications with clients and prospects, compensation, client funds and securities, and conflicts of interest.

We have elected to have three separate Units devoted to the Regulations with one large Unit on Ethical Practices.

PREPARING FOR THE EXAM

How Is the License Exam Manual Organized?

The License Exam Manual consists of Units (chapters) and Unit Tests organized to explain the material that NASAA has outlined for the exam. In addition to the regular text, each Unit also has some unique features designed to help with quick understanding of the material. When an additional point will be valuable to your comprehension, special notes are embedded in the text. Examples of these are included below.

TAKE NOTE   These highlight special or unusual information and amplify important points.

TEST TOPIC ALERT   Each Test Topic Alert! highlights content that is likely to appear on the exam.

EXAMPLE   These give practical examples and numerical instances of the material just covered and convert theory into practice.

You will also see Quick Quizzes, which will help ensure you understand and retain the material covered in that particular section. Quick Quizzes are a quick interactive review of what you just read.

Answers and rationale for the Quick Quizzes can be found at the end of each Unit.

The SecuritiesPro™ QBank includes a large bank of questions that are similar in style and content to those you will encounter on the exam. You may use it to generate tests by a specific topic or create exams that are similar in difficulty and proportionate mixture to the exam. One thing you should know about the SecuritiesPro™ QBank is that the answer choices are scrambled each time you take a test. That is, if the first time you saw a specific question, the correct answer was choice A, that statement might be choice D the next time.

Another important point is that the online questions are "live." That is, unlike this Manual, which, once printed can't be changed, our questions can be updated with a moment's notice. This enables us to keep current with rule changes and, to the extent possible, with new topics as they are added to the Series 63 exam. When we author questions covering material that is not in this Manual, there will be an asterisk (*) placed after the reference number indicating the general area where this topic belongs and that there is no specific information dealing with it other than this (or similar) questions.

Your study packet also includes an Online Practice Final. This is designed to closely simulate the true exam center experience in degree of difficulty and topic coverage and is an exceptional indicator of future actual exam score as well as areas of strength and weakness. When you have completed this exam, you will receive a detailed breakdown by topic of performance. This diagnostic breakdown will alert you to precisely where you need to concentrate further exam practice. It is important to note that you will only be able to take this exam *once* and will *not* be able to review the answers. This test is *not* for training purposes—it is to be taken shortly before your expected exam date and used as a tool to diagnose your readiness for the real exam.

If your study package includes a Mastery Exam, it, like the Practice Final, is to be used as a diagnostic tool and is taken after the Practice Final.

Other tools you should take advantage of include the following:

■ File of frequently asked questions (FAQs)—these are questions that previous students have submitted to our staff and contain detailed explanations that will be useful to you as you work your way through the material.

■ Exam-tips Blog and Test Alerts—our course editors frequently post items to their blog that relate to information about your exam. Please be sure to check the Blog regularly.

■ Study Calendar—design a calendar to help keep you on track.

Additionally, your study package may give you access to various topics from our video library. These short, engaging videos cover key topics from your manual. If your package includes access to our video library, please review the topics as you complete your reading assignment in the study manual.

What Topics Are Covered in the Course?

The License Exam Manual consists of 4 Units, each devoted to a particular area of study that you will need to know to pass the Series 63. Each Unit is divided into study sections devoted to more specific areas with which you need to become familiar. Please note that the first three Units apply to the 36 questions you will encounter on State Securities Acts and Related Rules and Regulations, and the fourth Unit covers the material found on the 24 questions on Ethical Practices.

The Series 63 License Exam Manual addresses the following topics:

Unit	Topic
1	Regulation of Persons
2	Regulations of Securities and Issuers
3	Remedies and Administrative Provisions
4	Ethical Practices and Fiduciary Obligations

How Much Time Should I Spend Studying?

Plan to spend approximately 20–30 hours reading the material and carefully answering the questions. Spread your study time over the 2–3 weeks before the date on which you are scheduled to take the Series 63 exam. Your actual time may vary depending on your reading rate, comprehension, professional background, and study environment.

What Is the Best Way to Structure My Study Time?

The following schedule is suggested to help you obtain maximum retention from your study efforts. Remember, this is a guideline only, because each individual may require more or less time to complete the steps included.

Step 1. Read a Unit and complete the Unit Test. Review rationales for all questions whether you got them right or wrong (2–3 hours per Unit).

Step 2. On the SecuritiesPro™ QBank, create and complete a test for each topic included under that Unit heading. For best results, it is better to do a large number of shorter tests than one or two longer ones. Carefully review all rationales. Do an additional test on any topic on which you score under 75%. After completion of all topic tests, create a 60-question test comprising all Unit topics. Repeat constructing 60-question tests until you score at least 75% (5–10 hours).

TAKE NOTE   Your score on the first attempt at any of these tests will give you an idea of how well you are absorbing the material. After all, when you take the actual exam, it will be your first look at those questions. It is important that you take the opportunity to learn from your mistakes and increase your knowledge, both of the material and test taking techniques.

Step 3. At this point, it is a good idea to begin creating 60-question tests covering all of the Units. Complete as many as necessary to achieve a score of at least 80–90%. Create and complete additional topic tests as necessary to correct problem areas (5–10 hours). There are more than enough questions in the QBank and while just taking tests is not the secret to passing the exam, exposing yourself to as many of these questions as you can increases the likelihood that you will see familiar items when you take your actual exam.

Step 4. The Online Practice Final mirrors the actual test in number of questions and subject matter coverage. Questions included in this exam are unique from all other question bank products, so you will see only new questions. Like the actual exam, you will not see the answer key and rationale, but the detailed diagnostic breakdown will provide you with clear guidance on areas where further study is required (1.5 hours).

How Well Can I Expect to Do?

The exams prepared by NASAA are not easy. You must display considerable understanding and knowledge of the topics presented in this course to pass the exam and qualify for registration.

If you study diligently, complete all sections of the course, and consistently score at least 85% on the tests, you should be well prepared to pass the exam. However, it is important for you to realize that merely knowing the answers to our questions will not enable you to pass unless you understand the essence of the information behind the question.

SUCCESSFUL TEST-TAKING TIPS

Passing the exam depends not only on how well you learn the subject matter, but also on how well you take exams. You can develop your test-taking skills—and improve your score—by learning a few test-taking techniques:

- Read the full question
- Avoid jumping to conclusions—watch for hedge clauses
- Interpret the unfamiliar question
- Look for key words and phrases

- Identify the intent of the question
- Memorize key points
- Avoid changing answers
- Pace yourself

Each of these pointers is explained below, including examples that show how to use them to improve your performance on the exam.

Read the Full Question

You cannot expect to answer a question correctly if you do not know what it is asking. If you see a question that seems familiar and easy, you might anticipate the answer, mark it, and move on before you finish reading it. This is a serious mistake. Be sure to read the full question before answering it—questions are often written to trap people who assume too much.

Avoid Jumping to Conclusions—Watch for Hedge Clauses

The questions on NASAA exams are often embellished with deceptive distractors as choices. To avoid being misled by seemingly obvious answers, make it a practice to read each question and each answer twice before selecting your choice. Doing so will provide you with a much better chance of doing well on the exam.

Watch out for hedge clauses embedded in the question. (Examples of hedge clauses include the terms *if*, *not*, *all*, *none*, and *except*.) In the case of *if* statements, the question can be answered correctly only by taking into account the qualifier. If you ignore the qualifier, you will not answer correctly.

Qualifiers are sometimes combined in a question. Some that you will frequently see together are *all* with *except* and *none* with *except*. In general, when a question starts with *all* or *none* and ends with *except*, you are looking for an answer that is opposite to what the question appears to be asking.

Interpret the Unfamiliar Question

Do not be surprised if some questions on the exam seem unfamiliar at first. If you have studied your material, you will have the information to answer all the questions correctly. The challenge may be a matter of understanding what the question is asking. In almost all cases, you can eliminate at least one and maybe two of the choices, thereby increasing your odds of success if you have to guess.

Very often, questions present information indirectly. You may have to interpret the meaning of certain elements before you can answer the question. Be aware that the exam will approach a concept from different angles.

Look for Key Words and Phrases

Look for words that are tip-offs to the situation presented. For example, if you see the word *prospectus* in the question, you know the question is about a new issue. Sometimes a question will even supply you with the answer if you can recognize the key words it contains. Few questions provide blatant clues, but many do offer key words that can guide you to selecting the correct answer if you pay attention. Be sure to read all instructional phrases carefully.

Take time to identify the key words to answer this type of question correctly.

Identify the Intent of the Question

Many questions on NASAA exams supply so much information that you lose track of what is being asked. This is often the case in story problems. Learn to separate the story from the question.

Take the time to identify what the question is asking. Of course, your ability to do so assumes you have studied sufficiently. There is no method for correctly answering questions if you don't know the material.

Memorize Key Points

Reasoning and logic will help you answer many questions, but you will have to memorize a good deal of information.

Avoid Changing Answers

If you are unsure of an answer, your first hunch is the one most likely to be correct. Do not change answers on the exam without good reason. In general, change an answer only if you:

■ discover that you did not read the question correctly; or

■ find new or additional helpful information in another question.

Pace Yourself

Some people will finish the exam early and some do not have time to finish all the questions. If you don't finish, you greatly reduce your chances of passing. Watch the time carefully (your time remaining will be displayed on your computer screen) and pace yourself through the exam.

Do not waste time by dwelling on a question if you simply do not know the answer. Make the best guess you can, mark the question for *Record for Review*, and return to the question if time allows. Make sure that you have time to read all the questions so that you can record the answers you do know.

THE EXAM

How Do I Enroll in the Exam?

To obtain an admission ticket to a NASAA exam, you or your firm must file an application form and processing fees with FINRA. To take the exam, you should make an appointment with a Prometric Testing Center as far in advance as possible of the date on which you would like to take the exam.

You may schedule your appointment at Prometric, 24 hours a day, 7 days a week, on the Prometric secure Website at **www.prometric.com**. You may also use this site to reschedule or cancel your exam, locate a test center, and get a printed confirmation of your appointment. To speak with a Prometric representative by phone, please contact the Prometric Contact Center at 1-800-578-6273.

What Should I Take to the Exam?

Take one form of personal identification with your signature and photograph as issued by a government agency. You cannot take reference materials or anything else into the testing area. Calculators are available upon request. Scratch paper and pencils will be provided by the testing center, although you cannot take them with you when you leave.

Exam Results and Reports

At the end of the exam, your score will be displayed, indicating whether you passed and including your scores on each testable exam area. The next business day after your exam, your results will be mailed to your firm and to the self-regulatory organization and state securities commission specified on your application.

1

Regulation of Persons

The Uniform Securities Act (USA) is model legislation designed to guide each state in drafting its state securities law. Questions on your Series 63 exam will be based on the 1956 version of the USA as well as the North American Securities Administrators Association's (NASAA) Statements of Policy and Model Rules. Although the USA is a template and not the law of any specific state, it is the basis for the questions on the exam.

In 1996, the US Congress enacted the National Securities Markets Improvements Act (NSMIA), national legislation designed to integrate securities markets and eliminate conflicting state and federal securities legislation. The definitions and regulations contained in this license exam manual reflect the changes to the USA required by the NSMIA. We will refer to the NSMIA from time to time, but the most important thing to remember at this time is that federal law (the power of the Securities Exchange Commission [SEC]), supersedes that of the state.

As the saying goes, "you can't tell the players without a scorecard." Neither can you understand the law without knowing the definitions of the key terms. In this particular Unit, it is critical to know the four classes of securities professionals and how they are regulated. The four classes are broker/dealers, agents, investment advisers, and investment adviser representatives. After a brief introduction to the important terms used in this Unit, we will come back to each of these four in greater detail.

The Series 63 exam will include 24 questions on the material presented in this Unit. ■

When you have completed this Unit, you should be able to:

- **identify** what is and what is not considered a *person*;

- **describe** the differences between exclusions from definitions and exemptions from provisions of the USA;

- **describe** the differences between broker/dealer, agent, investment adviser, and investment adviser representative;

- **recognize** the difference between a federal covered and a state registered investment adviser; and

- **identify,** for each category of professional, the procedures and requirements for registration in a state.

1. 1   DEFINITIONS UNDER THE UNIFORM SECURITIES ACT

1. 1. 1   THE UNIFORM SECURITIES ACT OF 1956 (USA)

1. 1. 1. 1   The USA is Model State Securities Legislation

With the enactment of numerous state securities laws, commonly referred to as blue-sky laws, the need for uniformity in securities laws among the states arose. In 1956, the **National Conference of Commissioners on Uniform State Laws (NCCUSL)**, a national organization of lawyers devoted to unifying state laws, drafted the original Uniform Securities Act **(USA)** as model legislation for the separate states to adopt. As model legislation, the USA is not actual legislation; the USA is a template or guide that each state uses in drafting its securities legislation. The securities laws of most states follow the USA very closely, and, in many cases, almost exactly.

TEST TOPIC ALERT   The exam will test your knowledge of the Uniform Securities Act, not the specifics of your state's securities legislation. The USA is periodically updated to adjust to developments in the securities markets through the passage of Model Rules. You will be tested on the 1956 version of the USA used by the **North American Securities Administrators Association (NASAA)**, the advisory body of state securities regulators responsible for the content of the exam. The Series 63 exam requires that you not only know what the USA says, but also are able to apply the law to concrete situations. General knowledge of the law is not enough to pass the exam; you will be asked to apply the law to situations that may arise in the course of business.

1. 1. 2   ADMINISTRATOR

Although some states may use other terms to describe this position, the exam will only use the word **Administrator** to refer to the office or agency that has the complete responsibility for administering the securities laws of the state.

Therefore, the Administrator has jurisdiction over all securities activity that emanates from his state as well as that received in his state. The Administrator has jurisdiction over the registration of securities professionals and securities. He has the power to make rules and issue orders. He can deny, suspend, or revoke registrations. Yes, there are some limitations on the Administrator's powers (and those will be covered in this Unit and Unit 4), but overall, this is one very powerful person.

When it comes to legal issues, terminology is critical. For example, there are three terms that will be used in this section that can become quite confusing. Let's try to explain them here, and they will make more sense as you go through this manual.

1. 1. 2. 1   Cease and Desist Order

This is used by the Administrator whenever it appears to him that any registered person has engaged or is about to engage in any act or practice constituting a violation of any provision of this act or any rule or order hereunder. The Administrator may issue a cease and desist order, with or without a prior hearing against the person or persons engaged in the prohibited activities, directing them to cease and desist from further illegal activity. Note that this only applies to registered persons, not securities.

1. 1. 2. 2   Stop Order

A **stop order** is used to deny effectiveness to, or suspend or revoke the effectiveness of, any registration statement. This applies only to securities, not professionals such as broker/dealers, agents, investment advisers and investment adviser representatives.

1. 1. 2. 3   Summary Order (Acting Summarily)

The dictionary defines "summarily" as acting without prior notice. This is one of the powers of the Administrator with regard to registration of both persons and securities. There are three specific cases where this power applies in the USA:

- Postponing or suspending the registration of any securities professional pending a final determination of a proceeding related to a problem
- Postponing or suspending the registration of a security pending a final determination of a proceeding relating to a problem
- Denying or revoking a specific security or transaction exemption

In each of these cases, upon the entry of the order, the Administrator must promptly notify all interested parties that it has been entered, the reasons for the order, and that within fifteen days after the receipt of a written request a hearing will be granted.

1. 1. 2. 4   Final Orders

Regardless of whether we're referring to persons, exemptions, or registration, other than in the case of a summary order, no final order may be entered without:

- appropriate prior notice to the interested parties;
- opportunity for hearing; and
- written findings of fact and conclusions of law.

1. 1. 3   BLUE-SKY LAWS

The common term used to refer to state securities laws.

1. 1. 4   PERSON

The term **person** means any individual, (sometimes known as a *natural person*), corporation, partnership, association, joint stock company, or trust where the interests of the beneficiaries are evidenced by a security, an unincorporated organization, a government, or a political subdivision of a government. This is a very broad definition.

Although there are a wide variety of entities that may be defined as persons, on the exam, there are only three nonpersons. Those are:

- minors (anyone unable to enter into contracts under the laws of the state);
- deceased individuals; and
- individuals legally declared mentally incompetent.

1. 1. 5   BROKER/DEALER

The term **broker/dealer** means any person engaged in the business of effecting transactions in securities for the account of others or for his own account. When acting on behalf of others, they are acting as brokers; when acting on behalf of themselves, they are acting as dealers. For exam purposes, it is critical to remember that the primary function of a broker/dealer is making securities transactions. In almost all cases, broker/dealers register with both the SEC and the state(s). This term is sometimes abbreviated to B/D on the exam.

1. 1. 6   AGENT

Agent means any **individual**, other than a broker/dealer, who represents a broker/dealer or issuer in effecting or attempting to effect purchases or sales of securities. You must know that these are always individuals (natural persons) and their function is to be involved in securities sales or supervising those who do. On FINRA exams, these individuals are referred to as registered representatives.

Almost always, these individuals work for broker/dealers, but, there can be instances when the individual is selling securities on behalf of the issuer of those securities.

1. 1. 7   INVESTMENT ADVISER

The term **investment adviser** means any person:

- who, for **compensation**, engages in the **business of advising** others, either directly or through publications or writings, as to the value of **securities** or as to the advisability of investing in, purchasing, or selling securities; or
- who, for compensation and as part of a regular business, issues or promulgates analyses or reports concerning securities.

Under the National Securities Markets Improvements Act of 1996 (NSMIA), investment advisers are registered with either the SEC (federal covered advisers) or the state (state covered adviser), but never both.

You may see the abbreviation IA on your exam.

1. 1. 8   INVESTMENT ADVISER REPRESENTATIVE

An **investment adviser representative** is any individual who represents a state-registered investment adviser or federal covered investment adviser performing duties related to the giving of or soliciting for advisory services.

1. 1. 9   ISSUER

The term **issuer** means any person who issues or *proposes* to issue any security. Issuers primarily include corporations and governments. However, under the USA, with respect to certificates of interest or participation in oil, gas, or mining titles or leases, or in payments out of production under such titles or leases, there is not considered to be any "issuer."

1. 1. 10   NONISSUER

The term **nonissuer** means not directly or indirectly for the benefit of the issuer.

1. 1. 11   SECURITY

The definition of **security** is quite broad and includes those items one normally thinks of as securities (e.g., stocks, bonds, debentures, mutual funds, variable annuities, etc.), but also includes a number of unusual items, such as an investment contract and a pre-organization certificate. We will cover securities in greater detail in the next Unit.

1. 1. 12   EXEMPT SECURITY

First, you must understand the meaning of the term **exempt**. When something is exempt, it means that it is excused from certain requirements. When a security is exempt under the USA, it does *not* have to be registered in order to be sold, and there are no requirements to file advertising about the security with the Administrator. You will see more in Unit 2.

1. 1. 13   EXEMPT TRANSACTION

Under the USA, an **exempt transaction** is one in which the nature of the sale is such that registration with the Administrator and filing of advertising material is *not* required in order for that transaction to take place. More to follow in the next Unit.

1. 1. 14   GUARANTEED

The term **guaranteed** means guaranteed as to payment of principal, interest, or dividends, but *not* capital gains.

1. 1. 15   OFFER/OFFER TO SELL

The terms **offer** and **offer to sell** include every attempt or offer to dispose of, or solicitation of an offer to buy, a security or interest in a security for value.

1. 1. 16 SALE

The term **sale** or **sell** includes every contract of sale of, contract to sell, or disposition of, a security or interest in a security for value. In other words, the offer is the attempt, the sale is when it is successful.

1. 1. 17 FRAUD

The term **fraud** means an intentional effort to deceive someone for profit; not limited to common-law deceit.

1. 1. 18 SRO

This is the abbreviation for **Self Regulatory Organization**. The most prominent of these is FINRA, but there are others such as the Municipal Securities Rulemaking Board (MSRB), the Chicago Board Options Exchange (CBOE), and the Investment Industry Regulatory Organization (IIRO) of Canada.

1. 1. 19 SOLICITOR

The term **solicitor** means any individual who, for compensation, acts as an agent of an investment adviser in referring potential clients. Solicitors must be registered as investment adviser representatives.

1. 1. 20 ACCREDITED INVESTOR

The term **accredited investor** is found in Rule 501 of the federal Securities Act of 1933. It refers to a person who is not counted when computing the number of investors purchasing a private placement under Regulation D of that Act. The term includes institutional investors such as banks, insurance companies, investment companies and large employee benefit plans; charitable organizations; corporations; or partnerships (total assets in excess of $5 million). In the case of natural persons (individuals), there are three ways to qualify:

- Be a director, executive level officer or general partner of the entity issuing the securities
- Having individual net worth, or joint net worth with the person's spouse, that exceeds $1 million at the time of the purchase, excluding the net equity of the primary residence of the person
- Having income exceeding $200,000 in each of the two most recent years or joint income with a spouse exceeding $300,000 for those years and a reasonable expectation of the same income level in the current year

Because it is a federal term, not one found in the Uniform Securities Act, on this exam, the term is basically used to confuse you as you will see when you go through our practice questions.

1. 1. 21 REGISTRANT

The term **registrant** is used in legal circles to refer to those securities professionals (B/Ds, IAs, agents, and IARs), or securities issuers, who are in the process of, or who have registered with the Administrator.

1. 1. 22 INSTITUTION

The term **institution** would include banks, trust companies, savings and loan associations, insurance companies, employee benefit plans with assets of not less than one million dollars ($1,000,000), and governmental agencies or instrumentalities. The Act generally affords less protection to these investors owing to their greater investment sophistication.

1. 1. 23 NATIONAL SECURITIES MARKETS IMPROVEMENTS ACT OF 1996 (NSMIA)

Congress enacted the NSMIA in 1996 to promote efficiency in capital formation in the financial markets. In effect, the act generally preempts states' blue-sky laws, eliminating the dual system of state and federal registration of certain securities and investment advisers.

1. 1. 24 STATE

The term **state** means any of the 50 states, any territory or possession of the United States (such as American Samoa and Guam), the District of Columbia, and Puerto Rico.

1. 2 BROKER/DEALERS AND AGENTS

Now that the basic terms used in the exam have been addressed, attention must now be directed to persons who are not excluded or exempted from provisions of the act. The following four classes of persons are included under the jurisdiction of state securities laws:

- Broker/dealers (generally legal persons such as corporations or partnerships)
- Agents (always individuals)
- Investment advisers (generally legal persons such as corporations or partnerships)
- Investment adviser representatives (always individuals)

Most of the attention on your exam will focus on broker/dealers and agents so we will begin with them.

TEST TOPIC ALERT   On your exam, always keep in mind which of the four categories of persons is the subject of the question. Rules that apply to agents, for example, are not the same as those that apply to broker/dealers. You will be tested on your understanding of the distinctions between each class of person defined in this Unit.

1. 2. 1   BROKER/DEALER

A **broker/dealer** is defined in the USA as any person (legal entity) engaged in the business of effecting transactions in securities for the accounts of others or for its own account. Any legal person (e.g., a securities firm) with an established place of business (an office) in the state that is in the business of buying and selling securities for the accounts of others (customers) and/or for its own proprietary account is a broker/dealer and must register in the state as such.

In other words, broker/dealers are firms for which registered representatives (agents) work. They are firms that engage in securities transactions, such as sales and trading. When acting on behalf of their customers—that is, buying and selling securities for their clients' accounts—broker/dealers act in an agency capacity. When broker/dealers buy and sell securities for their own accounts, called proprietary accounts, they act in a principal capacity as dealers.

TAKE NOTE   Individuals who buy and sell securities for their own accounts are not broker/dealers because they are engaged in personal investment activity, not the business of buying and selling securities for others. They are individual investors, not securities dealers.

TEST TOPIC ALERT   One of the roles of a broker/dealer is underwriting (distributing) shares of new securities for issuers. When they do that, they generally receive a commission on the sales, which they then use to pay their agents who actually made the sales to the clients.

1. 2. 1. 1   Exclusions from the Definition of Broker/Dealer

Broker/dealers are firms that buy and sell securities for others or themselves as a business. There are, however, many persons, legal and natural, that effect securities transactions that are excluded from the definition of broker/dealer for purposes of state regulation. Persons not included in the definition of broker/dealer are:

- agents;
- issuers; and
- banks, savings institutions, and trust companies (not engaged in broker/dealer activities).

Domestic commercial banks and other financial institutions are generally excluded from the definition of broker/dealer. However, with the adoption of the Gramm-Leach-Bliley Act in 1999, also known as the Financial Modernization Act, federal securities law adopted a functional approach to the regulation of financial institutions. Under the functional approach, financial institutions that engage in brokerage-related securities activities are subject to SEC registration as broker/dealers as well as to applicable provisions of state securities law—the USA—that relate to broker/dealers.

Today, most banks and other financial institutions engage in securities activities through broker/dealer subsidiaries. The broker/dealer subsidiaries of banks are, as a result, not excluded from the definition of a broker/dealer and therefore subject to the same securities regulations as other broker/dealers. Keep in mind that formation of these subsidiaries eliminates the need for the bank holding companies to register as broker/dealers. Their broker/dealer subsidiaries must, of course, register.

TAKE NOTE   Keep in mind the distinction between a bank holding company and a wholly owned commercial bank subsidiary. Commercial banks, the subsidiaries of bank holding companies, do not have to register because they are exempt. When engaged in securities transactions with the public, bank subsidiaries are subject to securities legislation as any other broker/dealer.

1. 2. 1. 1. 1   No Place of Business in the State

There is another exclusion from the definition of broker/dealer. This exclusion relates to the location of the broker/dealer's place of business. States exclude from the definition of broker/dealer those broker/dealers that:

- have no place of business in the state and deal exclusively with issuers, other broker/dealers, and other financial institutions, such as banks, savings and loan associations, trust companies, insurance companies, investment companies, and pension or profit-sharing trusts; and

- have no place of business in the state, but are licensed in a state where they have a place of business, and offer and sell securities in the state only with persons in the state who are existing customers and who are not residents of the state. This is sometimes referred to as the snowbird exemption and applies as well to agents, investment advisers, and investment adviser representatives.

In other words, the USA excludes broker/dealers with no place of business in the state from the definition of a broker/dealer to allow firms that deal exclusively with other broker/dealers and financial institutions to operate in the state without registering. The reason for this exclusion is that the regulators understand that this category of investor has a high level of investment sophistication and expertise and does not need the same degree of protection as the so-called "little guy."

The USA also allows broker/dealers to do business with existing customers who are temporarily in a state to avoid unnecessary multiple registrations. In most states, when an existing client legally changes residence to another state in which the broker/dealer is not registered, the firm has 30 days during which it may continue to do business with that client without registration in the new state. Should it wish to continue to maintain that client, the broker/dealer would have to register in that state.

As long as your client has not changed state of residence, there is no time limit. For example, many "snowbirds" spend the entire winter in Florida, which is no problem for the firms they do business with "up North." Or many people, after a couple of years in the workforce, decide to get an MBA. If they go out of state to a "resident" program for a year or two, that does not mean they've changed their state of residence, merely that they are not "commuter" students. Only when official residency is changed (new driver's license or voter registration) does the 30-day rule apply.

Notice how important language is here: if broker/dealers with no place of business in the state were defined as broker/dealers, they would be subject to state registration. If such broker/dealers with no place of business in the state are not defined as broker/dealers, however, those broker/dealers are not subject to the registration requirements of that state. Language and definitions determine jurisdiction. If a person or entity is defined as a broker/dealer, that person is covered by (subject to) the provisions of the act. If a person or entity is excluded from a definition, that person is not subject to (covered by) the act.

TEST TOPIC ALERT   The exam focuses more on the exclusions from the definition of broker/dealer than on the definition itself. Know these exclusions well.

CASE STUDY   **Exclusion from the Definition of Broker/Dealer**

Situation: First Securities Corporation is a registered broker/dealer with offices in Illinois. Mr. Thompson, a registered agent in the Illinois office of First Securities, recommends the purchase of ABC Shoes stock to his customer, Mr. Bixby, an Illinois resident, who is temporarily on vacation in Hawaii. Mr. Bixby agrees to the purchase of ABC Shoes, as well as other securities, while in Hawaii.

The Hawaiian state securities Administrator does not issue a cease and desist order against First Securities for unlawfully selling securities as an unregistered broker/dealer with an unregistered agent in Hawaii.

Analysis: The Hawaiian securities Administrator acted correctly by not issuing a cease and desist order against First Securities. Under the USA, First Securities is not required to register as a broker/dealer in Hawaii because it limits its business to an existing customer, Mr. Bixby, who is temporarily in the state. Because First Securities and Mr. Thompson are properly registered in Illinois, they need not register in Hawaii, provided, of course, Mr. Bixby does not take up permanent residence there. In this case, First Securities does not fall under the definition of broker/dealer in Hawaii because it does not do business in Hawaii other than with one existing customer temporarily in the state. In this situation, First Securities is not defined as a broker/dealer in the state of Hawaii, nor is Mr. Thompson defined as an agent, and therefore they do not have to register as a broker/dealer and agent in Hawaii. Definitions determine jurisdiction.

1. 2. 1. 2   Broker/Dealer Registration Requirements

Under the USA, if a person is included in the definition of broker/dealer, that person must register as a broker/dealer in the states where it does business. The USA is clear about broker/dealer registration. It states, "It is unlawful for any person to transact business in this state as a broker/dealer . . . unless he is registered under this act."

This means every person that falls within the definition of a broker/dealer must register with the Administrator of the state. Again, keep in mind that if a person falls under one of the exclusions from the definition, that person does not have to register in the state.

TEST TOPIC ALERT   In addition, at the time of registration of a broker/dealer, any partner, officer, or director of the broker/dealer is automatically registered as an agent of the broker/dealer. This does not mean that they don't have to take an exam. It just means that when a new broker/dealer is organized, these individuals submit information on the application that enables the Administrator to determine their eligibility for registration so a separate application does not have to be filed.

CASE STUDY   **Who Is a Broker/Dealer?**

Situation: First Securities Corporation of Illinois sells municipal bonds and equity securities to both the general public and other securities firms. First Securities sells many of its municipal bonds to its biggest customer, Transitions Broker/Dealers, Inc., located in Indiana. Transitions Broker/Dealers is a wholesale broker/dealer with no offices in Illinois that trades exclusively with other broker/dealers.

First Securities discovers that Transitions Broker/Dealers is not registered in Illinois but does business with other broker/dealers in Illinois. The president of First Securities asks the president of Transitions Broker/Dealers why his firm is not registered in Illinois; the president of Transitions answers that it is because they are not broker/dealers in Illinois. The president of First Securities is baffled—it appears to him that Transitions is indeed a broker/dealer.

Analysis: First Securities is a broker/dealer because it is a legal entity with a place of business in the state that effects securities transactions for itself and for the accounts of others and so must register in Illinois.

Like First Securities, Transitions Broker/Dealers conducts broker/dealer activities. However, in Illinois it confines the business to transactions between itself and other broker/dealers, such as First Securities. The USA specifically excludes from the definition of broker/dealer out-of-state broker/dealers who deal exclusively with other broker/dealers and have no place of business in the state.

Although Transitions Broker/Dealers is, in fact, conducting operations of a broker/dealer in Illinois, it does not meet the definition as stated in the USA and, therefore, is not subject to registration with the Illinois securities Administrator. If Transitions Broker/Dealers had a place of business in Illinois, it would be a broker/dealer by definition and would have to register as such in Illinois.

What about the Indiana Administrator? Which of the firms must register? Even though Transitions Broker/Dealers only trades with other broker/dealers, because it has an office in the state of Indiana, it would meet the definition of broker/dealer and would have to register as such. What about First Securities? Well, it depends on several factors we have not been told. Does First Securities maintain an office in Indiana? If it does, registration is required. If it does not and the only securities business it does is with other broker/dealers and financial institutions, it does not have to register in Indiana. However, if any of their clients are individuals (called retail clients on the exam), then registration is required.

1. 2. 1. 2. 1 Financial Requirements

The Administrator may establish net **capital requirements** for broker/dealers. Think of net capital as the broker/dealer's liquid net worth. Net capital requirements of the states may not exceed those required by federal law, in this case, the Securities Exchange Act of 1934. The Administrator of a state may require broker/dealers that have custody of, or discretionary authority over, clients' funds or securities to post **surety bonds**. The amount of the surety bond required by the states is limited to the amount set by the Securities Exchange Act of 1934. The Administrator may not require a bond of a broker/dealer whose net capital is in excess of that required by the SEC.

TEST TOPIC ALERT   You will have to know that broker/dealers who meet the SEC's net capital or bonding requirements *cannot* be required to meet higher ones in any state in which they do business.

TEST TOPIC ALERT   In lieu of a surety bond, the Administrator will accept deposits of cash or securities.

1. 2. 1. 2. 2   Effectiveness of Registration

Upon the applicant's submission of all required information to the state securities Administrator, the broker/dealer's registration becomes effective at noon on the 30th day after filing. The Administrator has authority to specify an earlier effective date as well as defer the effective date until noon of the 30th day after the filing of any amendment.

1. 2. 1. 2. 3   Registration Expiration

Broker/dealers' registrations expire on December 31 unless renewed.

QUICK QUIZ 1.A   True or False?

_____   1.   In general, a person who effects transactions in securities for itself or for the account of others in the course of business must register in the state as a broker/dealer.

_____   2.   Under the USA, an out-of-state firm that transacts business with an established customer who is on vacation is not considered a broker in the state in which the customer is on vacation.

_____   3.   A person not defined under the USA as a broker/dealer in the state need not register as such.

_____   4.   A broker/dealer registered in several states must meet the net capital standard of the state with the most stringent requirement.

Quick Quiz answers can be found at the end of the Unit.

1. 2. 2   AGENT

The USA defines an **agent** as any individual who represents a broker/dealer or an issuer in effecting (or attempting to effect) transactions in securities.

Agents are individuals in a sales capacity who represent broker/dealers or issuers of securities. As agents, they act, usually on a commission basis, on behalf of others. Other than on this exam, agents are usually referred to as registered representatives.

The use of the term *individual* here is important. Only an individual, or a natural person, can be an agent. A corporation, such as a brokerage firm, is not a natural person—it is a legal entity. The brokerage firm is the legal person (entity) that the agent (natural person) represents in securities transactions.

1. 2. 2. 1   Exclusions from Definition of Agent for Administrative Personnel

Clerical and administrative (sometimes referred to as *ministerial*) employees of a broker/dealer are generally not included in the definition of agent and, therefore, are not required to register. The logic for this exclusion from the definition should again be obvious. Clerical and administrative employees do not effect securities transactions with the public. They attend to the administration of the broker/dealer as a business organization. Under these circumstances, they are similar to employees of any other corporation. In fact, if the broker/dealer they work for wishes to pay their employees, including this group, a year-end bonus based on company profits (not related to any individual's sales efforts), it would be allowable.

The situation changes when administrative personnel take on securities-related functions. When they do so, they lose their exemption and must register as agents.

EXAMPLE
Secretaries and sales assistants are not agents if their activities are confined to administrative activities, including responding to an existing client's request for a quote or posting to client records. However, if secretaries or sales assistants accept customer transactions or take orders over the phone, they are engaging in securities transactions and are subject to registration as agents.

TEST TOPIC ALERT
"Cold callers" working for a broker/dealer would have to register as an agent if they did any more than ask if clients wanted to receive information. For example, if they pre-qualified clients or suggested ways to receive more money for their stocks or bonds, they would have to register as agents.

As is customary in other industries, broker/dealers frequently hire summer interns. If these interns received any selling related compensation, such as $10 for each existing client solicited, they would be considered agents and would have to register.

1. 2. 2. 2   Exclusions from the Definition of Agent for Personnel Representing Issuers

In many cases, individuals who represent issuers of securities are agents and therefore must register as such in the states in which they sell the issuers' securities. When does something like this occur? In many cases, a local company is looking to raise some additional capital—something in the range of several million dollars. Instead of going through the normal investment banking procedure (and paying all of those fees and commissions to the investment bankers), the company (known under the USA as the issuer), either uses its own employees or hires an outside sales force to sell the new security. However, individuals are excluded from the definition of agent and, therefore, are exempt from registration in a state when representing issuers in effecting transactions:

- in exempt securities;
- exempt from registration; and
- with existing employees, partners, or directors of the issuer if no commission or other remuneration is paid or given directly or indirectly for soliciting any person in this state.

1. 2. 2. 2. 1   Effecting Transactions in Exempt Securities

Securities exempt from registration are called **exempt securities**. An employee of an issuer is not an agent when representing an issuer of, for example, the following exempt securities:

- US government and municipal securities
- Securities of governments with which the United States has diplomatic relationships
- Securities of US commercial banks and savings institutions or trust companies (when not engaged in securities-related broker/dealer activities)
- Commercial paper rated in the top three categories by the major rating agencies with denominations of $50,000 or more and maturities of nine months or less
- Investment contracts issued in connection with an employee's stock purchase, savings, pensions, or profit-sharing plans

1. 2. 2. 2. 2   Effecting Exempt Transactions

An employee of an issuer is not an agent when representing an issuer in exempt transactions. Transactions exempt from registration are called **exempt transactions.** Some examples are:

- transactions between issuers and underwriters;
- transactions with institutions such as savings institutions or trust companies; and
- private placements.

TAKE NOTE
An employee of an issuer is not an agent when representing an issuer if the issue is exempt from registration (e.g., banks, financial institutions, and governments). Additionally, the employee is not an agent when representing an issuer in exempt transactions (transactions between an underwriter and issuer). Exempt securities and exempt transactions will be covered in detail in the next Unit.

TAKE NOTE
Keep in mind that an individual who works for an issuer of securities is excluded from the definition of agent when engaging in transactions with employees involving the issuer's securities, provided that the individual is not compensated for such participation by commissions or other remuneration based either directly or indirectly on the amount of securities sold. In other words, salaried employees engaged in distributing their employers' shares as part of an employee benefit plan would not be required to register as agents because they are by definition excluded from the definition. If such employees were compensated on the basis of the number of shares sold, they would be defined as agents and therefore would be subject to registration.

QUICK QUIZ 1.B Here are examples of questions you might see on the exam:

1. Under the Uniform Securities Act, the term *agent* would include an individual who represents an issuer in effecting non-exempt transactions in
   A. a city of Montreal general obligation bond
   B. common stock offered by a commercial bank
   C. a New Jersey Turnpike Revenue bond
   D. non-exempt securities

2. Under the Uniform Securities Act, the term *agent* would include
   A. an individual who represents an issuer in transactions in exempt securities
   B. an individual who represents a broker/dealer in a transaction in an exempt security
   C. a receptionist for a broker/dealer who directs calls for trade information to the appropriate individual
   D. the vice president of personnel for a national brokerage firm

1. 2. 2. 3 Agent Registration Requirements

The registration requirements for an agent who is not exempt are similar to those for a broker/dealer. The USA states, "It is unlawful for any person to transact business in this state as an agent unless he is registered under this act." In other words, an individual may not conduct securities transactions in a state unless that person is registered or exempt from registration in the state in which he conducts business. Furthermore, the act makes it unlawful for any broker/dealer or issuer to employ an agent unless the agent is registered.

The registration of an agent is not effective during any period when he is not associated with a particular broker/dealer registered under this act or a particular issuer. Therefore, if the broker/dealer's registration is terminated, the agent is no longer considered licensed. When an agent begins or terminates a connection with a broker/dealer or issuer, or begins or terminates activities that make him an agent, the agent and the broker/dealer or issuer must promptly notify the Administrator.

TAKE NOTE   When an agent shifts employment from one broker/dealer or issuer to another, all three persons—the agent, the old employer, and the new employer—must promptly notify the Administrator.

1. 2. 2. 3. 1 Financial Requirements

Unlike a broker/dealer, there are no financial requirements, or **net capital requirements**, to register as an agent. The Administrator may, however, require an agent to be bonded, particularly if the agent has discretion over a client's account.

CASE STUDY   **Agent as Defined by the USA**

> **Situation:** The City of Chicago issues bonds for the maintenance of local recreational facilities. Purchasers have two choices: they can purchase the bonds directly from the city through Ms. Stith (an employee of the city responsible for selling the bonds), or they can purchase them from Mr. Thompson (an employee of First Securities Corporation of Chicago). Neither Ms. Stith nor Mr. Thompson charges a commission, although First Securities is remunerated with an underwriting fee.
>
> **Analysis:** The City of Chicago is an issuer of exempt securities (municipal bonds). Ms. Stith, as an employee of the issuer (City of Chicago), is not an agent as defined in the USA because she is representing the issuer in the sale of an exempt security. Therefore, Ms. Stith does not need to register as an agent with the Administrator of Illinois. However, Mr. Thompson, as a representative of First Securities, must register with the Administrator because he represents a broker/dealer in effecting securities transactions in the state. Representatives (agents of broker/dealers) must register in the states in which they sell securities.

TAKE NOTE   Exemptions from registration generally apply to individuals who represent issuers, rather than to individuals who represent broker/dealers.

1. 2. 2. 3. 2   Fee and Commission Sharing

Registered agents of broker/dealers may share fees or split commissions with others provided they are registered as agents for the same broker/dealer or for a broker/dealer under common ownership or control. Interestingly enough, they can do this without disclosing the split to their clients. This is one of the very rare cases where disclosure is not necessary.

1. 2. 2. 3. 3   Multiple Registrations

An individual may not act at any one time as an agent for more than one broker/dealer or for more than one issuer, unless the broker/dealers or issuers for whom the agent acts are affiliated by direct or indirect common control or the Administrator grants an exception. In the event an agent does wish to affiliate with a second broker/dealer, the agent would have to go through the registration process with the second firm in the same manner as the original application.

1. 2. 2. 4   Limited Registration of Canadian Broker/Dealers and Agents

Provided the limited registration requirements enumerated below are met, a broker/dealer domiciled in Canada that has no office in this state may effect transactions in securities with or for, or attempt to induce the purchase or sale of any security by:

■ a person from Canada who is temporarily resident in this state and who was already a client of the broker/dealer; or

■ a person from Canada who is resident in this state and whose transactions are in a self-directed tax-advantaged retirement plan in Canada of which the person is the holder or contributor. In Canada, their equivalent of our IRA is called a Registered Retirement Savings Plan (RRSP).

An agent who will be representing a Canadian broker/dealer who registers under these provisions may effect transactions in securities in this state on the same basis as permitted for the broker/dealer.

For the Canadian broker/dealer to register in this fashion, it must:

- file an application in the form required by the jurisdiction where it has its principal office in Canada;
- file a consent to service of process;
- provide evidence that it is registered in good standing in its home jurisdiction; and
- be a member of an SRO or stock exchange in Canada.

Requirements for agents are the same, except that membership in an SRO or stock exchange is not relevant.

However, just as with domestic broker/dealers, if there is no place of business in the state, there are no registration requirements if the only securities transactions are with issuers, other broker/dealers, and institutional clients.

TAKE NOTE   Renewal applications for Canadian broker/dealers and agents who file for limited registration must be filed before December 1 each year.

QUICK QUIZ 1.C   Write **A** if the person is an agent and **B** if not.

_____ 1. A person who effects transactions in municipal securities on behalf of a broker/dealer

_____ 2. An agent's salaried secretary who takes buy and sell orders from clients

_____ 3. An employee of a bank whose job is selling securities issued by the bank

_____ 4. An individual who represents her nonexempt employer in the sale of its securities to existing employees for a commission

_____ 5. A person who represents an issuer in effecting transactions with underwriters

---

1. 3 INVESTMENT ADVISER

Under the USA, an **investment adviser** is defined as any person who, for compensation and as part of a regular business, engages in the business of advising others on the value of securities or on the advisability of investing in or selling them. The advice can be delivered in person, through publications or writings, or through research reports concerning securities.

Advice given on investments not defined as securities, such as rare coins, art, and real estate, is not investment advice covered by the USA or other securities legislation. As a result, persons providing such advice are not investment advisers. Again, definitions are crucial for determining whether an activity is subject to securities law.

To be an investment adviser under both state and federal securities law, a person must:

- provide advice about securities (not about jewelry, rare coins, or real estate);
- provide that advice as part of an ongoing business (hang a shingle and have an office for conducting business) on a regular basis; and
- receive compensation (payment for the advice).

TAKE NOTE   In most cases, investment advisers are legal persons, such as a partnership or corporation, that provide investment advice or portfolio management services on an ongoing basis. Investment adviser representatives work for investment advisers just as registered sales agents work for a broker/dealer. Note that an individual can be an investment adviser when the business is organized as a sole proprietorship.

1. 3. 1   SEC RELEASE IA-1092

As a result of the proliferation of persons offering investment advice, Congress directed the SEC to define the activities that would subject a person to the Investment Advisers Act of 1940. The SEC did so in SEC Release IA-1092. Because so much of the USA's interpretations dealing with investment advisers parallels the federal law, it is important to know how this Release has impacted the industry.

SEC Release IA-1092 interprets the definition of investment adviser under the Investment Advisers Act of 1940 to include financial planners, pension consultants, and others who offer investment advice as part of their financial practices.

Release IA-1092, in short, identifies as an investment adviser anyone who:

- provides investment advice, reports, or analyses with respect to securities;
- is in the business of providing advice or analyses; and
- receives compensation, directly or indirectly, for these services.

TAKE NOTE   If a person engages in these three activities, that person is an investment adviser subject to the Investment Advisers Act of 1940. As an investment adviser, this person must register with either the SEC or the states.

1. 3. 1. 1   Provide Investment Advice

In Release IA-1092, the SEC (and NASAA as well) maintains that a person who gives advice, whether in written or oral form, and issues reports, analyses, and recommendations about specific securities is an investment adviser if that person is in the business of doing so and receives compensation for the advice. This definition of investment adviser includes financial planners, pension consultants, and sports and entertainment representatives.

1. 3. 1. 1. 1   Financial Planners

Financial planners who make recommendations regarding a person's financial resources or perform analyses that concern securities are investment advisers if such services are performed as part of a business and for compensation. Under this interpretation, the SEC even includes financial planners who advise clients as to the desirability of investing in securities as an alternative to other investments, such as real estate, intangibles, or other assets.

1. 3. 1. 1. 2 Pension Consultants

Consultants who advise employee benefit plans on how to fund their plans with securities are also considered investment advisers by the SEC. In addition, under Release IA-1092, the SEC considers pension consultants who advise employee benefit plans on the selection, performance, and retention of investment managers to be investment advisers. A bit later in this Unit you will learn the conditions under which pension consultants become eligible to register with the SEC rather than the states.

1. 3. 1. 1. 3 Sports and Entertainment Representatives

Persons who provide financially related services to entertainers and athletes that include advice related to investments, tax planning, budgeting, and money management are also investment advisers.

TAKE NOTE
A sports agent who secures a favorable contract for a football player and receives a commission of 10% of the player's salary is not necessarily an investment adviser. However, if the sports agent advises the football player to invest his money in specific securities, the agent is then in the business of offering investment advice and would then be subject to the Investment Advisers Act of 1940 or the Uniform Securities Act.

1. 3. 1. 2 In the Business of Providing Advice

A person is in the business of providing advice and subject to regulation as an investment adviser if he:

- gives advice on a regular basis such that it constitutes a business activity conducted with some regularity (although the frequency of the activity is a factor, it is not the only determinant in whether one is in the business of giving advice, and providing advice does not have to be the person's principal activity); and
- advertises investment advisory services and presents himself to the public as an investment adviser or as one who provides investment advice.

TAKE NOTE
A person is in the business of giving investment advice if he receives separate compensation that represents a charge for giving the advice.

A person is in the business if he provides investment advice or issues reports on anything other than rare, isolated, and nonperiodic instances. In this context, a person is an investment adviser if he recommends that a client allocate funds to specific assets, such as high-yield bonds, technology stocks, or mutual funds.

A person whose business is to offer only nonspecific investment advice, through publication of a general newsletter, for example, is not covered by the act. However, such a person would be included if he acted as a representative of a broker/dealer and then made specific securities recommendations to clients.

1. 3. 1. 3   Compensation

A person who receives an economic benefit as a result of providing investment advice is an investment adviser. The compensation can be direct or indirect. Compensation includes advisory fees, commissions, and other types of fees related to the service rendered. A separate fee for the advice need not be charged; the fee can be paid by a third party on behalf of the beneficiary of the advice.

EXAMPLE

Fees that an investment adviser receives from a corporation for advice given to the corporation's employees or retirees are considered compensation. A financial planner who designs a comprehensive financial plan for the corporation's employees without charging a fee but receives commissions on insurance policies sold as part of the plan is acting as an investment adviser representative. Even though that compensation is indirect, it meets the Release's definition of compensation for investment advice.

1. 3. 2   EXCLUSIONS FROM THE DEFINITION OF INVESTMENT ADVISER

As is the case with broker/dealers and agents, there are exclusions from the term *investment adviser*. If a person is excluded, none of the registration requirements apply. Under the USA, the following are not investment advisers. They are excluded from the definition:

■ Investment adviser representatives (the business entity is the investment adviser, not the representative)

■ Banks, savings institutions, and trust companies

■ Lawyers, accountants, teachers, and engineers (LATE) whose investment advisory services are solely incidental to their professional practices

This exclusion is not available to any of the above professionals who have established a separate advisory business. Also, the exclusion would not apply to any of the above who holds himself out as offering investment advice.

The following also are excluded from the definition:

■ Broker/dealers whose investment advisory services are incidental to their brokerage business and who receive no special or separate compensation for offering advice

Why is that broker/dealers qualify for this exclusion? Including this exception in the law amounts to a recognition that brokers/dealers commonly give a certain amount of advice to their customers in the course of their regular business, and that it would be inappropriate to bring them within the scope of the definition of an IA merely because of this aspect of their business. On the other hand, reference to *special compensation* amounts to an equally clear recognition that a broker/dealer who is specially compensated for the rendition of advice should be considered an investment adviser and not be excluded from the purview of the Act merely because he is also engaged in effecting market transactions in securities. It is well known that many brokers/dealers have investment advisory departments which furnish investment advice for compensation in the same manner as does an investment adviser who operates solely in an advisory capacity. The essential distinction to be borne in mind in considering borderline cases is the distinction between compensation for advice itself and compensation for services of another character to which advice is merely incidental.

■ A publisher, employee, or columnist of a newspaper, news magazine, or business or financial publication of regular and general circulation; or an owner, operator, producer, or employee of a cable, radio, or television network, station, or production facility if, in either case, the financial or business news published or disseminated is made available to the general public and the content does not consist of rendering advice on the basis of the specific investment situation of each client

Although most newsletter publishers are excluded, if the publication schedule is "event generated" (i.e., reports are issued as a result of certain market events), then the exclusion is lost and registration would be necessary.

■ Federal covered investment advisers registered with the SEC (advisers with $30 million or more in assets under management or under contract to a registered investment company)
■ Any other person the Administrator specifies

Sometimes the exam will refer to *exceptions* rather than *exclusions*. Both terms mean the same thing for test purposes.

1. 3. 2. 1   Federal Covered Advisers

The NSMIA made major changes in the way investment advisers register. The NSMIA divided registration responsibilities between the SEC and the states' securities departments. Basically, the largest firms are required to register with the SEC, and the smaller ones are required to register with the states. Unlike broker/dealers, who almost always register with the SEC and one or more states, investment advisers are registered with one or the other, never both.

Advisers registered with the SEC are known as **federal covered investment advisers**. Federal covered advisers are those:

- required to be registered or registered as an investment adviser with the SEC;
- under contract to manage an investment company registered under the Investment Company Act of 1940, regardless of the amount of assets under management; or
- excluded from the definition of an investment adviser by the Investment Advisers Act of 1940.

TAKE NOTE   Because so much of this exam deals with interpreting the laws, it is sometimes necessary to review some legal concepts. For example, if a person is excluded from the definition of investment adviser under the Investment Advisers Act of 1940, the states, under the NSMIA, cannot define such person as an investment adviser because federal law excluded that person from the definition. In other words, if the separate states could define the persons who were excluded from the federal definition as investment advisers, the federal law would have no meaning.

The NSMIA established a cutoff point based upon assets under management (AUM). This was further expanded under the Dodd-Frank Wall Street Reform and Consumer Protection Act of 2010. Dodd-Frank contains three levels—small, mid-size, and large. Small advisers, those with less than $25 million in AUM, will, with rare exception, always register with the state(s). Mid-size, those with at least $25 million in AUM, but less than $100 million in AUM, will, with a few more exceptions, also register on the state level. Once the $100 million in AUM level is reached, an investment adviser becomes eligible for SEC registration.

The SEC recognized that market conditions (or obtaining or losing clients) can cause AUM to fluctuate so they established a buffer to keep advisers from having to switch back and forth. The numbers work like this. A state registered adviser may, once it has assets under management of at least $100 million (subject to certain exceptions; everyone needs at least $100 million to initiate registration with the SEC), choose to remain state registered or may register with the SEC. Once AUM reach $110 million, registration with the SEC is mandatory—they can no longer stay state registered. Then, once registered with the SEC, an investment adviser need not withdraw its SEC registration unless it has less than $90 million of assets under management. This means that an investment adviser can register with the SEC with AUM of as little as $100 million, but must once AUM reach $110 million. Likewise, those investment advisers registered at the state level, can choose to remain there until they reach the $110 million level. The determination is made when filing the annual updating amendment to the ADV. If at $110 million or more, SEC registration is required. Once SEC registered, If AUM remains at $90 million or more, SEC registration may be maintained. If under $90 million, unless qualifying for an exception, registration with the state(s) is required. Go below $90 million and a Form ADV-W must be filed and the investment adviser has 180 days to register with the appropriate state(s). This buffer is designed to avoid the expense and hassle involved in potentially annual changes to where the investment adviser is registered. Related to this is the requirement that Pension Consultants must have at least $200 million in AUM to be eligible to be federal covered.

Investment advisers exempt from state registration are not exempt from paying state filing fees and giving notice to the Administrator. The procedure is called **notice filing.**

TEST TOPIC ALERT   As part of the notice filing procedure, the Administrator can require the federal covered investment adviser to submit copies of ALL documentation filed with the SEC and, of course, pay a filing fee.

TAKE NOTE   If a federal covered adviser only deals with institutions, other IAs, other B/Ds, and so forth, notice filing is not required. This is a similar concept to the USA not requiring registration of state covered advisers who have no place of business in the state and deal with this same group of clients. We have not heard of this ever being asked on the exam, but, you never know what NASAA has up their sleeve.

As a general rule, the SEC or federal rules involve bigger numbers than the state rules—large investment advisers must register with the SEC; small and mid-size investment advisers must register with the state.

Adviser managing . . .

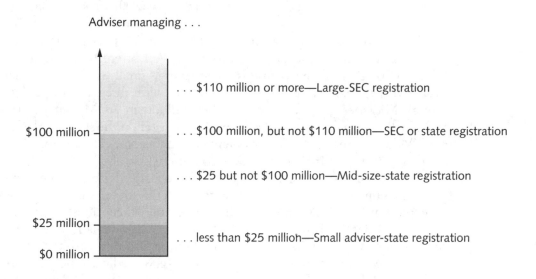

. . . $110 million or more—Large-SEC registration

$100 million — . . . $100 million, but not $110 million—SEC or state registration

. . . $25 but not $100 million—Mid-size-state registration

$25 million —

$0 million — . . . less than $25 million—Small adviser-state registration

TEST TOPIC ALERT   An investment adviser registered under state law whose assets reach $110 million under management has 90 days to register with the SEC. A federal covered investment adviser whose assets under management fall below $90 million no longer qualifies for SEC registration and has 180 days to register with the state(s).

1. 3. 3   EXEMPTION FROM REGISTRATION FOR INVESTMENT ADVISERS

The USA exempts from registration certain persons who, although included in the definition of investment adviser, do not have to register as such in the state. These exemptions from registration are advisers who have no place of business in the state but are registered in another state, provided their only clients in the state are:

- broker/dealers registered under the act;
- investment advisers;

- institutional investors, including large employee benefit plans;
- existing clients who are not residents but are temporarily in the state (e.g., "snowbirds");
- limited to five or fewer clients, other than those listed above, resident in the state during the preceding 12 months (called the de minimis exemption); or
- any others the Administrator exempts by rule or order.

TAKE NOTE

Because these exemptions all apply when the investment adviser does not have an office in the state, it is relevant to understand that an investment adviser or one of its representatives who advertises to the public, in any way, the availability of meeting with prospective clients in a hotel, seminar, or any other location in the state is considered to have an office in the state. However, an investment adviser representative who contacts clients in the state and notifies them that he will be passing through their town and is available to meet with them in his hotel room is not considered to have an office in the state because the announcement is being made only to existing clients and not to the public. If the IAR asks clients to bring their friends, the exemption is lost.

TEST TOPIC ALERT

The de minimis provision applies only to IAs and IARs, not to broker/dealers or agents.

CASE STUDY

Out-of-State Advice

Situation: A California-registered investment adviser with no offices located in any other state has directed investment advice over the past year to five individual residents of the state of Nevada. Is the investment adviser required to register in the state of Nevada?

Analysis: The answer is no. Registration is not required because the investment adviser does not have an office in Nevada and directs business to five or fewer individual residents of the state during the year. If the firm had an office in Nevada, registration would be required in that state. Also, even if the firm had no office in Nevada, registration would be required if business had been transacted with six or more individual residents of the state during the previous 12 months.

If the business had been transacted with other investment advisers, broker/dealers, or institutional investors, there is no limit as long as there is no office in the state.

Situation: Charles & Goode, a partnership located in Illinois, has been in the business of selling investment advice in the form of research reports and managing securities portfolios for the past 20 years. The partnership has earned a good reputation among investors and has managed less than $100 million until this year. This year, they gained several new clients and now have $120 million in assets under management.

Most of Charles & Goode's clients are wealthy individuals and residents of Illinois, but they have 3 individual clients who are residents of Wisconsin and 30 non-institutional clients who live in Indiana. The principals of Charles & Goode have also formed a separate partnership called C&G Mutual Fund Advisers, Inc., which manages a small registered investment company with assets of $15 million. The partners of Charles & Goode are uncertain about what they must do to be in compliance with the registration requirements of the USA.

Analysis: As a partnership in the business of managing money for individual clients, Charles & Goode is included in the definition of investment adviser and must register as such with the Illinois securities Administrator until it manages $100 million or more in assets. However, with the addition of new clients as of the current year, Charles & Goode will be exempt from registration with Illinois, as it is now excluded from the definition of investment adviser. Charles & Goode is now a federal covered adviser that must register with the SEC because it has crossed the threshold of $110 million in assets under management. As a federal covered adviser, the firm would be required to do a notice filing if requested by the Administrator.

Before becoming a federal covered adviser, Charles & Goode need not register in Wisconsin because they have five or fewer clients in the state; however, they had to register in Indiana because they have more than five clients there. After becoming federal covered advisers, Charles & Goode does not have to register in Indiana, Wisconsin, or Illinois; after it manages more than $110 million, it only has to register with the SEC, not state Administrators. An adviser with assets of at least $100 million but not $110 million may register with either the state or the SEC. Advisers with $110 million or more in assets under management must register with the SEC only.

The separate partnership, C&G Mutual Fund Advisers, Inc., which manages only $15 million, is exempt from registration in Illinois (or any other state) because persons who operate as investment advisers to investment companies registered under the Investment Company Act of 1940, regardless of the size of the investment company, are federal covered advisers not subject to state registration. Both C&G Mutual Fund Advisers Inc., and the fund they manage may have to pay state filing fees under a procedure called **notice filing**.

1. 3. 4   REGISTRATION REQUIREMENTS FOR AN INVESTMENT ADVISER

The registration requirements for an investment adviser are much like those for a broker/dealer. The USA states, "It is unlawful for any person to transact business in this state as an investment adviser. . . unless he is so registered under this act or is exempt as described above from a state's registration requirements." In other words, persons included in the definition of investment adviser must register in the states in which they do business unless they are exempt from registration.

1. 3. 4. 1   Form ADV

The application for registration as an investment adviser is on the Form ADV. There are four parts to this form: Parts 1A and 1B and Parts 2A and 2B.

Part 1 contains information about the IA, including:

- location of principal office;
- location of books and records (if not at the principal office);
- form of business organization (sole proprietorship, partnership, corporation);
- method of business;
- other business activities (broker/dealer, registered representative of a B/D);
- maintaining custody of customer assets or exercising discretion;
- details relating to all control persons (officers, directors, partners, etc.); and
- disciplinary history.

Part 1B asks additional questions required by state securities authorities. Federal covered advisers do not complete the Part 1B.

Part 2A is known as the investment adviser's brochure and tends to focus on customer related information, such as:

- compensation arrangements (fees, commissions, hourly charge);
- types of clients (individuals, institutions, pension plans);
- type of investments (equities, corporate debt, municipal securities, US treasuries, investment companies);
- types of strategies employed (buy and hold, value, growth);
- methods of analysis used (technical, fundamental); and
- educational and business background of those who render advice.

The brochure is arranged in a narrative form using plain English.

Part 2B requires advisers to create brochure supplements containing information about certain supervised persons. Together, Part 2A and Part 2B are delivered to the client as described later in Unit Four.

State covered advisers file *both* Part 1 and Part 2 with the Administrator of each state in which they are registering.

TEST TOPIC ALERT   Under the USA, if a federal covered investment adviser has an office in the state, the Administrator may require, by rule or by order, that the IA submit any documents that have been filed with the SEC. A federal covered IA submits only Part 1A of the Form ADV. Therefore, if the Administrator requests the Form ADV, all that will be sent is the Part 1A. If it is a state covered adviser, then the Administrator can request Parts 1A and 1B.

QUICK QUIZ 1.D

1. Under the USA, the definition of investment adviser would include
   A. a bank
   B. a lawyer charging a fee to advise clients how to invest an injury settlement he just won for them
   C. an investment adviser representative
   D. none of the above

1. 3. 4. 2   Financial Requirements

The Administrator may, by rule or order, establish minimal financial requirements for an investment adviser registered in the state (state covered). The Administrator may require an adviser who has custody of or discretionary authority over client funds or securities to post bonds or another form of security. Usually, the bond is higher for custody than for discretion. Typically, the bond required of investment advisers with discretionary authority is $10,000, whereas advisers maintaining custody of customer funds and/or securities will need a bond or net worth of $35,000. In lieu of the surety bond, the Administrator will generally accept cash or marketable securities.

The USA specifies the action to be taken by a registered investment adviser whose net worth falls below the required minimum. By the close of business on the next business day, the adviser must notify the Administrator that the investment adviser's net worth is less than the minimum required. After sending that notice, the adviser must file a financial report with the Administrator by the close of business on the next business day.

TEST TOPIC ALERT

Because the USA is only a template, some states have higher net worth or bonding requirements. The exam may want you to know that if a state covered IA meets the net worth or surety bonding requirements for the state where its principal office is located, that is sufficient in any other state in which it may be registered.

TEST TOPIC ALERT

One of the effects of the NSMIA is to limit the powers of an Administrator over a federal covered adviser, particularly one whose principal office is in another state. Section 222 of the Investment Advisers Act of 1940 would prohibit an Administrator from conducting an audit of a federal covered adviser unless the adviser's principal office is located in that state. Another limitation is that any financial or bonding requirements, as well as rules relating to recordkeeping, are solely under federal jurisdiction when it comes to federal covered advisers.

TEST TOPIC ALERT

The proper term to use when referring to the financial requirements of an investment adviser is *net worth* while for broker/dealers, it is *net capital*. However, we have heard from a number of students that NASAA is using net capital where they should be using net worth in questions about IAs. So, if you want to get the question right, answer it the way they give it to you. You will see several examples of this in our practice questions.

Write **A** if the phrase describes an investment adviser that must register under the USA and **B** if it does not.

_____ 1. Publisher of a newspaper that renders general financial advice

_____ 2. Broker/dealer that charges a fee for providing investment advice over and above commissions from securities transactions

_____ 3. Investment adviser that manages $10 million in assets

_____ 4. Publisher of a monthly investment newsletter with an annual subscription fee that does not render specific advice based on the needs of any subscriber

1. 3. 4. 3 Wrap Fee Programs

The exclusion offered to broker/dealers is lost when the brokerage firm earns special compensation for giving advice. One of the most common examples is the wrap fee program. In this type of asset management program, the broker/dealer wraps all of its services together, including transactions, advice, custody, and research, for one flat fee, usually a percentage of assets under management.

Because the wrap fee includes payment for securities advice, generally, the broker/dealer must be registered as an investment adviser and any agent participating must be registered as an investment adviser representative.

Firms offering these programs must make several critical disclosures to their clients, including:

■ the amount of the wrap fee charged for the program;

■ whether the fees are negotiable;

■ the services provided under the program, including the types of portfolio management services;

■ a description of the nature of any fees that the client may pay in addition to the wrap fee; and

■ a statement that the program may cost the client more than purchasing these services separately (it is important that you remember this final disclosure for the exam).

1. 3. 4. 4 Fiduciary

A fiduciary is a person legally appointed and authorized to hold assets in trust for another person. The fiduciary manages the assets for the benefit of the other person rather than for his or her own profits and must exercise a standard of care imposed by law. Examples include an executor of an estate, a trustee, and, in this exam, an investment adviser. It is because of this fiduciary responsibility that NASAA has prepared a Statement of Policy dealing solely with investment adviser activity.

1. 4 INVESTMENT ADVISER REPRESENTATIVE

Investment adviser representative (IAR) means any partner, officer, director (or an individual occupying a similar status or performing similar functions), or other individual employed by or associated with an investment adviser that is registered or required to be registered under the Uniform Securities Act (state covered IA). If employed by or associated with a federal covered adviser, this individual only comes under the registration requirements by having a place of business in the state. In both cases (state or federal), the individual meets the definition of an IAR by doing any of the following:

- Makes any recommendations or otherwise renders advice regarding securities
- Manages accounts or portfolios of clients
- Determines which recommendation or advice regarding securities should be given
- Solicits, offers or negotiates for the sale of or sells investment advisory services
- Supervises employees who perform any of the foregoing

TAKE NOTE

The use of the term *individual* here is important. Only an individual, or a natural person, can be an investment adviser representative. The investment advisory firm is the legal person (entity) that the IAR (natural person) represents in performing the above listed functions.

1. 4. 1 REGISTRATION REQUIREMENTS FOR INVESTMENT ADVISER REPRESENTATIVES

It is unlawful for any state covered investment adviser to employ an investment adviser representative unless the investment adviser representative is registered under this act. However, the registration of an investment adviser representative is not effective during any period when he is not employed by an investment adviser registered under this act. The same holds true for a federal covered adviser to employ, supervise, or associate with an investment adviser representative having a place of business located in this state, unless such investment adviser representative is registered under this act, or is exempt from registration.

TEST TOPIC ALERT

The effect of the previous statement (found in Section 203A of the Investment Advisers Act of 1940), is that for those performing as IARs for federal covered advisers, state registration is required only in those states where that individual has a place of business. Place of business of an investment adviser representative means:

(1) an office at which the investment adviser representative regularly provides investment advisory services, solicits, meets with, or otherwise communicates with clients; and

(2) any other location that is held out to the general public as a location at which the investment adviser representative provides investment advisory services, solicits, meets with, or otherwise communicates with clients.

Registration of an investment adviser also leads to automatic investment adviser representative registration of partners, officers, or directors active in the business and anyone else performing a similar function. What does that really mean? An investment adviser representative can only be registered as a representative of a registered adviser, so individuals holding the positions mentioned above are in limbo until the adviser's registration becomes effective. At that time, their individual registrations go into effect. Instead of filing a Form U-4 or Form U-10, their personal information is included in the Form ADV Part 1 filed by the investment adviser. And, just like any other IAR, they must take and pass the appropriate qualification exam(s).

For those of you who have taken a FINRA exam, you know there is a supervisory level of registration—registered principal. No such gradations apply under NASAA rules. So, no matter how high ranking the officer (of either a B/D or IA), he just registers as either an agent or an IAR.

Many independent financial planners operate as independent contractors, not employees of investment advisory firms or broker/dealers. Regardless, they are required to be registered as investment adviser representatives of the firm and must be placed under the same level of supervisory scrutiny as employees. Their business cards may contain the name of their separate planning entity, but must also disclose the name of the entity registered as the investment adviser.

TEST TOPIC ALERT   Registered investment advisers are responsible for the supervision of individuals registered as investment adviser representatives, but acting in the capacity of independent contractors, to the same extent that they supervise those who are actual employees of the firm.

Investment Adviser: Business or Individual

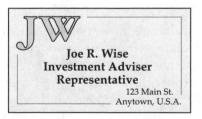

Investment Adviser Representative:
Individual Only

1. 4. 1. 1   Financial Requirements of IARs

Unlike an investment adviser, there are no financial requirements, or net worth requirements, to register as an investment adviser representative. The Administrator may, however, similar to an agent for a B/D, require an IAR to be bonded, particularly if the representative has discretion over a client's account.

1. 4. 2   EXCLUSIONS FROM THE DEFINITION OF INVESTMENT ADVISER REPRESENTATIVE

Employees of investment advisory firms are excluded from the term *investment adviser representative*, provided their activities are confined to clerical duties or those activities that are solely incidental to the investment advisory services offered. Should the investment advisory employee receive specific compensation for offering these services, the employee would then have to register as an investment adviser representative. Exclusion criteria for administrative employees of investment advisers are much like those for administrative personnel of broker/dealers.

TAKE NOTE   Although not specifically tested, you should know that to become an investment adviser representative, one must pass either the NASAA Series 65 or Series 66 exam. In some jurisdictions, a FINRA exam, such as the Series 6 or Series 7, must also be completed.

1. 4. 3   INVESTMENT ADVISER REPRESENTATIVE TERMINATION PROCEDURES

When an investment adviser representative begins or terminates employment with an investment adviser, the investment adviser (in the case of one registered with the state) or the investment adviser representative (in the case of one federal covered), shall promptly notify the Administrator.

1. 5 SUMMARY OF THE FOUR SECURITIES PROFESSIONALS

Now that we have completed defining the four categories of securities professionals, here is an explanatory summary. Many students, particularly those without any securities background, seem to have a problem sorting out who is who. Perhaps the following will help.

A **broker/dealer** is a business entity. From a legal standpoint, this entity may be organized as a sole proprietorship but, in the real world, there are less than a handful of FINRA members who are. Virtually every B/D is a corporation, partnership, or LLC. The primary business function of every broker/dealer is the **execution of securities transactions**, either for their clients or for their own accounts. These firms hire individuals, known on this exam as agents, to work for them. You may have heard the term stockbroker, registered rep, account executive, and so forth, but on this exam, they are only called agents.

The role of an **agent** is to represent his or her employer (the broker/dealer) in working with clients or supervising those who do. Upon completing the registration requirements, including passing this exam, a person will be an agent.

An **investment adviser**, like a broker/dealer, is a business entity. Unlike a broker/dealer, there are a number of IAs who are organized as sole proprietorships. There is a reason for this, but totally unrelated to anything you will ever have to know for the exam. Still, most investment advisers are structured as corporations, partnerships, or LLCs. The primary function of every investment adviser is, as the name implies, to give **investment advice**. They do *not* engage in securities transactions—that is the role of a B/D.

Just as broker/dealers hire individuals (agents) to work for them, investment advisers hire individuals, known as **investment adviser representatives**, to represent them in the rendering of investment advice. Once again, we have an employer/employee relationship.

There are many firms that are registered as both broker/dealers and and investment advisers. Therefore, there are many individuals who are agents as well as IARs. These are two different roles and perform different functions. Hopefully, this summary makes it clear what these are.

TEST TOPIC ALERT

Registration of a broker/dealer leads to automatic agent registration of partners, officers, or directors active in the business and anyone else performing a similar function. Registration of an investment adviser also leads to automatic investment adviser representative registration of the same category of persons. Don't be confused by the term *similar function*. Here is NASAA's explanation for it: *The phrase "any person occupying a similar status or performing similar functions," which modifies "partner, officer, or director" here and elsewhere in the Act, contemplates unincorporated, non-partnership organizations like Massachusetts trusts.* This is just some more legalese you might encounter on the exam. Please note that not all officers, directors, and so forth, get automatically registered; only those who are performing a function that requires them to be registered as agents or IARs will automatically get registered.

QUICK QUIZ 1.F

True or False?

_____ 1. An investment adviser representative must register with the SEC if she has clients with assets of $110 million or more under management.

_____ 2. An investment adviser maintaining custody of a customer's securities or funds and exercising discretion in the account is generally required to maintain a minimum net worth of $35,000.

_____ 3. An employee of an investment advisory firm is an investment adviser representative if his duties are limited to clerical activities.

_____ 4. An administrative employee who receives specific compensation for offering investment advisory services is not an investment adviser representative.

_____ 5. An employee of an investment advisory firm is an investment adviser representative if his duties involve making investment recommendations.

6. Under the USA, the term *investment adviser representative* would NOT include

A. an officer of a registered investment advisory firm whose responsibility includes supervision of solicitors

B. an associated person of the firm who, from time to time, makes specific recommendations to clients

C. a payroll clerk employed by an advisory firm whose responsibilities include computing the earnings of investment adviser representatives

D. a new employee of an advisory firm who has only been able to sign up 2 clients in his first 4 months

1. 6 GENERAL REGISTRATION PROCEDURES

Any person who meets the definition of broker/dealer, agent, investment adviser, or investment adviser representative must register with the state. To register with the state securities Administrator, such persons must:

■ submit an application;

■ provide a consent to service of process;

■ pay filing fees;

■ post a bond (if required by the Administrator); and

■ take and pass an examination if required by the Administrator, which may be written, oral, or both.

TEST TOPIC ALERT   Please note that, unlike FINRA (NASD) registration requirements, fingerprints do not have to be submitted.

1. 6. 1   SUBMITTING AN APPLICATION

All persons must complete and submit an initial application (as well as renewals) to the state securities Administrator. The application must contain whatever information the Administrator may require by rule and may include:

■ form and place of business (broker/dealers and investment advisers);

■ proposed method of doing business;

■ qualifications and business history (broker/dealers and investment advisers must include the qualifications and history of partners, officers, directors, and other persons with controlling influence over the organization);

■ court issued injunctions and administrative orders within the past 10 years;

■ adjudications by the SEC or any securities SRO within the past 10 years;

■ convictions within the past 10 years of misdemeanors involving a security or any aspect of the securities business;

■ felony convictions within the past 10 years, whether securities related or not;

■ financial condition and history (broker/dealers and investment advisers only, but only of the firm—no credit reports on the officers);

- any information to be furnished or disseminated to any client or prospective client, if the applicant is an investment adviser; and
- in the case of an individual registrant, (agent or investment adviser representative) citizenship information.

The Administrator also may require that an applicant publish an announcement of the registration in one or more newspapers in the state.

TEST TOPIC ALERT   If an agent terminates employment with a broker/dealer, both parties must notify the Administrator promptly.

If an agent terminates employment with Broker/Dealer A to join Broker/Dealer B, all three parties must notify the Administrator. If an investment adviser representative terminates employment with an investment adviser, notification requirements depend on how the investment adviser is registered.

If the investment adviser is a state-registered adviser, the firm must notify the Administrator. If the investment adviser is a federal covered adviser, the investment adviser representative must notify the Administrator.

1. 6. 2   PROVIDE CONSENT TO SERVICE OF PROCESS

New applicants for registration must provide the Administrator of every state in which they intend to register with a consent to service of process. The **consent to service of process** appoints the Administrator as the applicant's attorney to receive and process noncriminal securities-related complaints against the applicant. Under the consent to service of process, all complaints received by the Administrator have the same legal effect as if they had been served personally on the applicant.

TAKE NOTE   The consent to service of process is submitted with the initial application and remains in force permanently. It does not need to be supplied with each renewal of a registration.

1. 6. 3   PAYMENT OF INITIAL AND RENEWAL FILING FEES

States require filing fees for initial applications as well as for renewal applications. If an application is withdrawn or denied, the Administrator is entitled to retain a portion of the fee. Filing fees for broker/dealers, investment advisers, and their representatives need not be identical. Broker/dealers or investment advisers may file, without a fee, an application for registration of a successor firm, whether or not the successor is then in existence, for the unexpired portion of the year.

The renewal date for all registrations is December 31, and there is no proration of fees. In the case of broker/dealers and investment advisers, a successor firm (an entity that acquires or takes over the operation of the existing firm) pays no fees until the renewal date.

No matter when the initial registration occurs, renewal is always the *next* December 31. For example, if you register on September 22, 2010, your license will come up for renewal December 31, 2010.

1. 6. 4   POST-REGISTRATION REQUIREMENTS

The USA requires registered broker/dealers and investment advisers to keep accounts, blotters (records of original entry), correspondence (including emails), memoranda, papers, books, and other records the Administrator requires. These records must be preserved for three years by broker/dealers and five years by investment advisers unless the Administrator prescribes otherwise.

All records must be readily accessible (in the principal office) for the first two years.

The Administrator may also require registered broker/dealers and investment advisers to file financial reports. As noted previously, for SEC registered broker/dealers or investment advisers, the recordkeeping and financial reports required by the state Administrator may not exceed those required by the Securities Exchange Act of 1934 or the Investment Advisers Act of 1940.

If any material information in these documents becomes inaccurate or incomplete, the registrant must promptly file a corrected copy (*amend* their application) with the Administrator. All required documents are subject to reasonable periodic, special, or other examination as the Administrator deems appropriate, in the public interest, or for the protection of the investor.

Although it is required to keep all records relating to customers, there are no requirements to keep copies of their **tax returns**.

There is another recordkeeping requirement that may be the subject of an exam question. Partnership articles and any amendments, articles of incorporation, charters, minute books, and stock certificate books of the investment adviser and of any predecessor, shall be maintained in the principal office of the investment adviser and preserved until at least **three** years after termination of the enterprise.

1. 6. 4. 1   Maintenance and Preservation of Records

How may these records be kept and preserved by the broker/dealer or investment adviser? The records required to be maintained and preserved may be maintained and preserved for the required time by a broker/dealer or an investment adviser on:

- paper or hard copy form, as those records are kept in their original form;
- micrographic media, including microfilm, microfiche, or any similar medium; or
- electronic storage media, including any digital storage medium or system that meets the terms of this section.

The firm must:

- arrange and index the records in a way that permits easy location, access, and retrieval of any particular record;

■ provide promptly any of the following that the Administrator may request

    — a legible, true, and complete copy of the record in the medium and format in which it is stored,

    — a legible, true, and complete printout of the record, and

    — means to access, view, and print the records; and

■ separately store, for the time required for preservation of the original record, a duplicate copy of the record on any medium allowed by the rules.

In the case of records created or maintained on electronic storage media, the firm must establish and maintain procedures:

■ to maintain and preserve the records, so as to reasonably safeguard them from loss, alteration, or destruction;

■ to limit access to the records to properly authorized personnel and the Administrator; and

■ to reasonably ensure that any reproduction of a non-electronic original record on electronic storage media is complete, true, and legible when retrieved.

1. 6. 4. 1. 1   The Effect of the NSMIA Upon Post Registration Requirements

The NSMIA amended the Securities Exchange Act of 1934 by adding a section which reads as follows:

> *No law, rule, regulation, or order, or other administrative action of any State or political subdivision thereof shall establish capital, custody, margin, financial responsibility, making and keeping records, bonding, or financial or operational reporting requirements for broker/dealers that differ from, or are in addition to, the requirements in those areas established under this Act.*

And the NSMIA added a section to the Investment Advisers Act of 1940 which states:

> *No law of any state or political subdivision thereof requiring the registration, licensing, or qualification as an investment adviser or supervised person of an investment adviser shall apply to any person (A) that is registered under federal law as an investment adviser, or that is a supervised person of such person, except that a State may license, register or otherwise qualify an investment adviser representative that has a place of business located within that State; or (B) that is not registered under federal law because that person is excluded from the definition of an investment adviser under the Act.*

The effect of this on broker/dealers (who largely register with both the SEC and the States), is that all financial, bonding, and recordkeeping requirements are basically those of the SEC, and the states can't do anything about that. In the case of investment advisers, if the IA is federal covered, no state regulations will apply other than the requirement to register IARs.

TEST TOPIC ALERT   Keeping up with current trends, the exam is likely to ask about retention requirements for electronic communications, specifically email. Email has the same requirements as any other documents: three years for broker/dealers and five years for investment advisers. Emails from a registered person that are strictly of a personal nature and not to a client ("Honey, I'll be late for dinner," or, "I'll pick up the kids after basketball practice") do not have to be retained.

TEST TOPIC ALERT   Because the Uniform Securities Act is only a template, some states have more stringent recordkeeping requirements than others. The exam will want you to know that as long as a state covered investment adviser complies with the requirements of the state in which its principal office is located, it will not have to meet the requirements of any other state. Remember, federal covered advisers comply only with SEC rules.

TAKE NOTE   To avoid unnecessary duplication of examinations, the Administrator may cooperate with the securities Administrators of other states, the SEC, and any national securities exchange or national securities association registered under the Securities Exchange Act of 1934.

TEST TOPIC ALERT   The Administrator's authority does not stop at the state line. The Administrator, or his representative, of any state in which the person is registered may demand an inspection of any of these books and records during reasonable business hours with whatever frequency the Administrator deems necessary.

1. 6. 5   EFFECTIVENESS OF REGISTRATION

Unless a legal proceeding is instituted or the applicant is notified that the application is incomplete, the license of a broker/dealer, agent, investment adviser, or investment adviser representative becomes effective at noon 30 days after the later of the date an application for licensing is filed and is complete or the date an amendment to an application is filed and is complete. An application is complete when the applicant has furnished information responsive to each applicable item of the application. By order, the Administrator may authorize an earlier effective date of licensing. The Administrator will notify the employing firm of effectiveness, and they will tell the new registrants when they are "good to go."

In the same manner as a registration becomes effective on the 30th day after application, a request to withdraw registration also becomes effective on the 30th day after submission. However, should there be any legal proceedings in progress, the withdrawal will be held up until resolution of the issue. In any event, once withdrawal has taken place, the Administrator has jurisdiction of the former registrant for a period of one year.

TEST TOPIC ALERT   Although withdrawal of registration normally takes 30 days, the Administrator has the power to shorten that period, in effect permitting a rush order.

TEST TOPIC ALERT

While registration as an agent or IAR is pending, the individual may not take part in any activity that would require registration. Clerical work or assisting with research would be permitted.

QUICK QUIZ 1.G

1. Under the USA, which of the following automatically becomes registered as an agent when a broker/dealer registration becomes effective?

    A. Only the designated supervisory principal
    B. Any partner, officer, or person of similar status or similar function
    C. All agents currently registered with FINRA through that broker/dealer
    D. No one

2. Under the USA, which of the following statements regarding the registration of a successor firm is(are) TRUE?

    A. The appropriate filing fee must be included with the application.
    B. The successor firm must be in existence before the filing of the application.
    C. The registration of the successor firm will be effective until the December 31 renewal date.
    D. All of the above.

3. A non-federal covered investment adviser whose principal office is located in State A is also registered in States B and C. The IA maintains custody of client funds and securities. Which of the following statements are CORRECT?

    I. The IA must meet the net worth requirements of State A regardless of the requirements of State B or State C.
    II. The IA must meet the highest net worth requirements of State A, B, or C.
    III. The IA must keep records in accordance with the requirements of State A, regardless of the requirements of State B or State C.
    IV. The IA must keep records in accordance with the requirements of each state in which it is registered.

    A. I and III
    B. I and IV
    C. II and III
    D. II and IV

QUICK QUIZ 1.H

True or False?

____ 1. A consent to service of process must be submitted with each renewal application.

____ 2. An Administrator may establish net capital requirements for investment adviser representatives.

____ 3. When a securities professional registers in a state, he must provide the state Administrator with a list of all states in which he intends to register.

UNIT TEST

1. Which of the following would be an agent under the terms of the USA?

 I. A sales representative of a licensed broker/dealer who sells securities in the secondary markets to the general public
 II. An assistant to the president of a broker/dealer who, for administrative purposes, accepts orders on behalf of the senior partners
 III. A subsidiary of a major commercial bank registered as a broker/dealer that sells securities to the public
 IV. An issuer of nonexempt securities registered in the state and sold to the general public

 A. I and II
 B. I, II and III
 C. III and IV
 D. I, II, III and IV

2. A publicly traded corporation offers its employees an opportunity to purchase shares of the company's common stock directly from the issuer. A specific employee of the company is designated to process orders for that stock. Under the USA, the employee

 A. must register as an agent of the issuer
 B. need not register as an agent of the issuer under any circumstances
 C. may receive commissions without registration
 D. must register as an agent if he will receive commissions or remuneration either directly or indirectly

3. Registration as an investment adviser would be required for any firm in the business of giving advice on the purchase of

 A. convertible bonds
 B. gold coins
 C. rare convertible automobiles
 D. apartments undergoing a conversion to condominiums

4. Under the Uniform Securities Act, which of the following requires registration as an investment adviser representative?

 A. An employee, highly skilled in evaluating securities, who performs administrative or clerical functions for an investment adviser
 B. An individual who renders fee-based advice on precious metals
 C. A solicitor for an investment advisory firm who is paid a fee for his services
 D. An agent of a broker/dealer who offers incidental advice on securities as part of his sales commissions

5. Under the Uniform Securities Act, all of the following may provide investment advice incidental to their normal business without having to register as an investment adviser EXCEPT

 A. a teacher
 B. an economist
 C. a lawyer
 D. an engineer

6. Which of the following persons is defined as an agent by the Uniform Securities Act?

 A. Silent partner of a broker/dealer
 B. Secretary of a branch office sales manager
 C. Clerk at a broker/dealer who is authorized to take orders
 D. An officer of a broker/dealer who does not solicit or transact securities business

7. Under the Uniform Securities Act, any partner, officer, or director of a registered investment adviser is an investment adviser representative if he

   I. offers advice concerning securities
   II. manages client accounts or portfolios
   III. determines securities recommendations for representatives to disseminate
   IV. supervises personnel engaged in the above activities but does not sell these services to the public

   A. I only
   B. I and II
   C. I, II and III
   D. I, II, III and IV

8. Under the Uniform Securities Act, an agent is a(n)

   A. broker/dealer who sells registered securities to the general public
   B. individual who represents an investment adviser
   C. individual representing a broker/dealer who sells securities exempt from registration under the act
   D. individual who represents an issuer in an exempt transaction

9. For purposes of the definition found in Rule 501 of Regulation D of the Securities Act of 1933, the term *accredited investor* would not apply to

   A. an investment adviser representative
   B. an investment company registered under the Investment Company Act of 1940
   C. an officer of the company involved in the underwriting
   D. a large employee benefit plan

10. Under the Uniform Securities Act, an investment adviser is all of the following EXCEPT

   I. a broker/dealer who charges for investment advice
   II. a publisher of a financial newspaper
   III. a person who sells security analysis
   IV. a CPA who, as an incidental part of her practice, suggests tax-sheltered investments to her affluent clients

   A. I and II
   B. II and III
   C. II and IV
   D. III and IV

11. Under the Uniform Securities Act, the term *person* would include all of the following EXCEPT

   I. an unincorporated association
   II. a child prodigy, gifted in math, in the custody of his parents, for whom his parents opened an account at a major securities firm
   III. a political subdivision
   IV. an individual

   A. I, II and IV
   B. II only
   C. II and III
   D. III and IV

12. Under the USA, which of the following is considered a broker/dealer in a state?

   A. First Federal Company Trust
   B. XYZ broker/dealer with an office in the state whose only clients are insurance companies
   C. An agent effecting transactions for a broker/dealer
   D. A broker/dealer with no place of business in the state who only does business with other broker/dealers

13. Which of the following must register as an agent?

   A. An individual representing a broker/dealer who sells commercial paper
   B. An individual who sells commercial paper for ABC National Bank
   C. An employee of the Fed whose job is selling Treasury bonds to the public
   D. An individual who is paid a commission to sell certificates of deposit for ABC National Bank

14. An investment adviser hires 2 individuals to solicit new customers for the firm's wealth management service. Under the USA
    A. they may begin soliciting as soon as they have passed their licensing examinations
    B. soliciting is generally prohibited
    C. each of them would have to register as an investment adviser
    D. registration as investment adviser representatives is required

15. Which of the following would meet the definition of investment adviser under the Uniform Securities Act?
    I. A broker/dealer charging separately for investment advice
    II. The publisher of a weekly magazine, sold on newsstands, that contains at least 5 stock recommendations per issue
    III. A civil damages attorney who advertises that he is available to assist clients by suggesting appropriate investments for their successful claims
    IV. A finance teacher at a local community college who offers weekend seminars on comprehensive financial planning at a very reasonable price
    A. I only
    B. I, II and III
    C. I, III and IV
    D. I, II, III and IV

16. The term *investment adviser representative* would NOT include
    I. an employee of an investment adviser whose sole responsibility is filing paid bills and similar documents
    II. a receptionist operating the switchboard at the office of an investment adviser
    III. a minority stockholder whose only activity was soliciting new clients
    IV. the operator of the word processing equipment used as a desktop publishing system to prepare the adviser's weekly list of recommendations
    A. I and II
    B. I, II and III
    C. I, II and IV
    D. III only

17. With regard to state covered investment advisers, all of the following statements regarding the powers of the Administrator are true EXCEPT
    A. the Administrator may request submission of literature used by the adviser to solicit new business
    B. the Administrator must be provided with a detailed description of the adviser's proposed method of selecting investments
    C. an investment adviser's registration must be renewed each December 31st
    D. the Administrator may rule that custody of client funds is not permissible

18. An investment adviser, having no place of business in the state, would be exempt from registration under the Uniform Securities Act if her only clients were
    I. banks or other financial institutions
    II. investment companies
    III. accredited investors
    A. I and II
    B. I and III
    C. II and III
    D. I, II and III

19. Which of the following statements regarding a broker/dealer's withdrawal of registration under the Uniform Securities Act are TRUE?
    I. Unless a proceeding is involved, withdrawal will become effective 30 days after application unless the Administrator elects to shorten the period.
    II. Unless a proceeding is involved, withdrawal will be effective 30 days after application unless the Administrator elects to lengthen the period.
    III. Once withdrawal becomes effective, the Administrator can no longer commence an action against the former broker/dealer.
    IV. If an action is commenced against the broker/dealer after application for withdrawal is filed, but before the 30th day, effectiveness of the withdrawal is withheld until resolution of the action.
    A. I and III
    B. I and IV
    C. II and III
    D. II and IV

20. An investment adviser is exempt from registration under the Uniform Securities Act if he has no place of business in the state and his only clients are

    I. banks
    II. insurance companies
    III. individuals who are residents of that state and none of his advice deals with securities traded on a national exchange
    IV. accredited investors

    A. I and II
    B. I, II and III
    C. I, II and IV
    D. I, II, III and IV

21. An investment adviser would be exempt from registration under the Uniform Securities Act if she had no place of business in the state and

    I. she offered her services to no more than 5 individuals in that state during any consecutive 12-month period
    II. she offered her services to fewer than 15 individuals in that state during any consecutive 12-month period
    III. her only clients were registered investment companies
    IV. her only clients were broker/dealers and other investment advisers

    A. I and III
    B. I, III and IV
    C. II and III
    D. II and IV

22. During the application process for registration as an agent, the Administrator may request information about the applicant's

    I. annual income
    II. citizenship
    III. record involving a securities related misdemeanor conviction 5 years ago
    IV. proposed method of doing business

    A. I, II, III and IV
    B. II, III and IV
    C. II and III
    D. I and IV

23. A broker/dealer is registered in State X. It has no offices in State Y, although it does do business in that state. Under the Uniform Securities Act, registration in State Y is required if the client is a(n)

    A. bank
    B. broker/dealer
    C. insurance company
    D. investment adviser representative

24. Which of the following terms are synonymous?

    I. Salesman/Agent
    II. Dealer/Salesman
    III. Dealer/Agent

    A. I only
    B. I and II
    C. I and III
    D. II and III

25. Your primary source of earnings is the commissions generated on purchases and sales of securities by your customers. On occasion, you sell some of your clients mutual funds with 12b-1 fees, and, as a result, quarterly trails are paid to you even though no further money is being invested. Under the Uniform Securities Act

    A. you would be required to be registered as an investment adviser representative because your share of these asset-based fees would be considered special compensation
    B. you would be required to be registered as an investment adviser as your share of these asset-based fees would be considered special compensation
    C. this is permissible as long as you are currently licensed as an agent
    D. no further registration is necessary as long as the proper disclosures are made in the wrap fee disclosure document

ANSWERS AND RATIONALES

1. **A.** Under the USA, only individuals can be agents. A person who sells securities for a broker/dealer is an agent. An administrative person, such as the assistant to the president of a broker/dealer, is considered an agent if he takes securities orders from the public. Corporate entities are excluded from the definition of agent. Broker/dealers and issuers are not agents.

2. **D.** Under the USA, an individual is an agent when effecting transactions with an issuer's existing employees if commissions are paid. Therefore, there are cases where the employee would have to register as an agent.

3. **A.** Only persons in the business of giving advice on securities are required to register as investment advisers. Only the convertible bonds are securities.

4. **C.** A solicitor is considered an investment adviser representative under the Uniform Securities Act. An employee who performs only clerical or administrative functions is not an investment adviser representative. Precious metals are not securities; therefore, a person advising on them is not considered an investment adviser representative. An agent is a representative of a broker/dealer, and, as long as the only form of compensation is sales commissions, registration as an investment adviser representative is not required.

5. **B.** The Uniform Securities Act does not exclude economists from the definition of investment adviser as it does lawyers, accountants, teachers, and engineers who give advice that is incidental to the practice of their profession. Remember the acronym LATE—lawyers, accountants, teachers, and engineers. Test takers often mistake the E in LATE for economist.

6. **C.** Anyone who solicits or receives an order while representing a broker/dealer is an agent. Silent partners and administrative personnel are not agents under the terms of the USA if they do not solicit or receive orders. As long as the officer has no supervisory role, or other active participation in the securities business of the broker/dealer, the USA does not consider this position to require registration as an agent. An example might be the Vice-President of Human Resources. Remember, broker/dealers are not agents; agents represent broker/dealers. If, however, any of these individuals were authorized to accept orders, registration as an agent would be required.

7. **D.** The Uniform Securities Act defines persons associated with an investment adviser as investment adviser representatives, including any partner, officer, or director who offers advice concerning securities. Persons who manage client accounts or portfolios, determine securities recommendations, or supervise personnel engaged in the above activities are investment adviser representatives.

8. **C.** An individual employed by a broker/dealer who sells securities to the public is an agent under the Uniform Securities Act. The USA defines an agent as "any individual other than a broker/dealer who represents a broker/dealer or issuer in effecting or attempting to effect purchases or sales of securities." The law excludes from the definition of agent individuals who represent an issuer in exempt transactions, the sale of exempt securities, and transactions with issuers' employees when no commission is paid. There is virtually no case in which a salesperson representing a broker/dealer is not an agent.

9. **A.** An individual is not an accredited investor solely by virtue of being an IAR. If that person had the net worth or income specified in the Rule, that would be okay, but just being in the business does not qualify someone.

10. **C.** A publisher of a financial newspaper and a CPA who, as an incidental part of her practice, suggests tax-sheltered investments are not investment advisers.

11. **B.** The term *person* is extremely broad. Excluded from the term would be a minor, a deceased individual, and one who has legally been determined incompetent.

12. **B.** Any broker/dealer with an office in the state, regardless of the nature of its clients, is defined as a broker/dealer under the USA. If the firm did not have an office in the state and its only clients were institutions (such as insurance companies) or other broker/dealers, it would be excluded from the definition. Banks or trust companies and agents are never broker/dealers.

13. **A.** An individual who represents a broker/dealer and sells any security must register under the USA. The securities (commercial paper) are exempt; nevertheless, the representative must be registered as an agent of the broker/dealer. An individual who sells commercial paper for ABC National Bank would not have to register because the bank is excluded from the definition of broker/dealer. An employee of the federal government need not register with the state because he represents an exempt issuer. An individual who is paid a commission to sell certificates of deposit for a commercial bank does not have to register as an agent because he is not selling a security.

14. **D.** The definition of investment adviser representative includes individuals who solicit for the firm's advisory business.

15. **C.** Publishers of general circulation newspapers and magazines are excluded from the definition of investment adviser, even if the entire publication is devoted to investment advice. A broker/dealer loses its exclusion the moment it offers advice for a separate charge, as does an attorney who holds himself out as offering investment advice. Normally, a teacher is excluded, but not when charging for advice, as would appear to be the case here. On this examination, the term *comprehensive financial planning* always includes securities advice.

16. **C.** Clerical and administrative employees are not considered to be investment adviser representatives. Minority stockholder or not, someone involved in soliciting accounts would be an investment adviser representative.

17. **B.** It is not required that an investment adviser disclose to the Administrator the methods he uses to select investments.

18. **A.** Do not be mislead by the term *accredited investor*. It has absolutely no meaning other than when referring to a private placement of securities under the Securities Act of 1933. This term will appear frequently on the exam out of context (i.e., unrelated to private placements). Whenever it does, you can make the question easier by replacing the term with the phrase *ordinary public investor who needs all of the protection available under the law*. As long as the adviser has no place of business in the state, she is exempt from registration if her only clients are institutional investors such as banks, insurance companies, investment companies, other investment advisers, broker/dealers, $1 million or larger employee benefit plans, college endowment funds, and governmental units.

19. **B.** Withdrawal of registration normally becomes effective 30 days after application. The Administrator may shorten that period but may not lengthen it unless an action against the B/D is commenced. Once an action is commenced, withdrawal may not take effect until resolution of the case. The Administrator may take action against any registrant for up to 1 year after withdrawal.

20. **A.** An adviser with no place of business in the state is exempt if his clients are institutional (banks, insurance companies, investment companies, and so forth). But, when the securities are sold to non-institutional clients who are residents of the state, registration is required. The term *accredited investor* has no meaning here because it applies only to private placements under Regulation D of the Securities Act of 1933. This term will appear frequently on the exam out of context (i.e., unrelated to private placements). Whenever it does, you can make the question easier by replacing the term with the phrase *ordinary public investor who needs all of the protection available under the law.*

21. **B.** To enable an investment adviser to service a small number of clients in neighboring states without the hassles of registration, the de minimis requirements allow offers to up to 5 persons, other than institutional accounts, during any 12-month period. There is no limit to the number of institutional clients (e.g., investment companies and broker/dealers) an out-of-state adviser can have and still be exempt from registration in that state.

22. **B.** The Administrator asks all registrants about their proposed method of doing business. Individual registrants may be asked about their citizenship. Securities related misdemeanors within the past 10 years are relevant. The earnings of an agent are not within the purview of the Administrator and are not pertinent to an applicant for registration.

23. **D.** Broker/dealers must always register in a state if they do business with noninstitutional clients, regardless of the nature of the individual's employer.

24. **A.** *Agent* is another term for registered representative or salesman. An agent cannot be a broker/dealer; he can only work for one.

25. **C.** Even though we commonly associate fees with investment advice, the 12b-1 fee charged by some mutual funds is not considered to be the special compensation the law refers to when requiring registration as either an investment adviser or adviser representative. This is not a wrap fee program.

QUICK QUIZ ANSWERS

Quick Quiz 1.A

1. **T.**   A person who effects transactions in securities for itself or for the account of others must register in the state as a broker/dealer unless specifically excluded from the definition.

2. **T.**   A firm with an out-of-state registration is not considered a broker/dealer in that state if transacting business with a customer who is passing through the state on vacation.

3. **T.**   If a person is excluded from the definition, that person need not register as a broker/dealer; however, if not excluded, the person must register.

4. **F.**   Any broker/dealer registered in several states is also going to be registered with the SEC. Under the NSMIA, federal law always "trumps" state law so the only requirement to be met is that of the SEC.

Quick Quiz 1.B

1. **D.**   As long as the individual represents the issuer in a transaction involving exempted securities, he is not included in the definition of agent , even when the transaction is non-exempt. But, when the securities themselves are non-exempt, and the transactions are non-exempt, the individual is defined as an agent. And, yes, you may see this many "negatives" in a single question. Notice that a 19-month commercial paper is not exempt, but the other choices are.

2. **B.**   Most of the exclusions from the term *agent* refer to an individual representing an issuer. There is almost no case where an individual performing a sales function for a broker/dealer is not an agent. Clerical persons are not agents, nor are officers with no apparent sales function.

Quick Quiz 1.C

1. **A.**   Persons must be registered as agents when they effect transactions on behalf of broker/dealers whether the securities are exempt or not.

2. **A.**   Any individual taking orders on behalf of a broker/dealer must be registered whether or not they receive a commission.

3. **B.**   An employee who represents an issuer of exempt securities (a bank) in selling its securities does not register as an agent because such an individual is not an agent under the USA.

4. **A.**   A person who represents an employer in selling securities to employees must register as an agent if the person receives a commission. If no commission is paid, registration is not necessary.

5. **B.**   Persons who represent issuers in securities transactions with underwriters need not register as agents because this is an exempt transaction.

Quick Quiz 1.D

1. **B.**   Although lawyers are generally excluded from the definition of investment adviser, that exclusion holds true only if the advice given is solely incidental to the practice of the profession and no separate fees are charged. The separate billing here is what loses the exclusion. Remember, investment adviser representatives are not investment advisers, just as agents are not broker/dealers.

Quick Quiz 1.E

1. **B.** Publishers of newspapers and magazines of general circulation that offer general financial advice need not register.

2. **A.** Broker/dealers must register as investment advisers if they receive special or separate compensation for giving investment advice.

3. **A.** An investment adviser that manages less than $100 million in assets must register as an investment adviser under the USA. If the client is an investment company registered under the Investment Company Act of 1940, registration with the SEC is mandatory regardless of amount under management.

4. **B.** The exclusion pertaining to securities advisory publishers includes newsletter publishers who do not give advice to subscribers on the subscriber's specific investment situation and who publish on a regular basis.

Quick Quiz 1.F

1. **F.** An investment adviser (not the investment adviser representative) must register with the SEC if the firm manages assets of $110 million or more. The individual would have to be registered as an investment adviser representative in the state(s) in which she does business with retail clients.

2. **T.** An investment adviser maintaining custody of customer funds or securities must have a net worth of at least $35,000 regardless of whether or not the firm exercises discretion.

3. **F.** An employee of an investment advisory firm is not an investment adviser representative if his duties are confined to clerical activities.

4. **F.** Any employee who receives specific compensation for offering investment advisory services is considered an investment adviser representative.

5. **T.** Any employee of an investment advisory firm is an investment adviser representative if his duties involve making investment recommendations.

6. **C.** Clerical and administrative personnel are excluded from the definition of investment adviser representative. Remember, the definition includes anyone who makes recommendations (even if only upon occasion), manages accounts, solicits accounts, or supervises any of the above.

Quick Quiz 1.G

1. **B.** All individuals with management responsibility at the firm are automatically registered as agents when a broker/dealer becomes registered in a state, including officers, directors, and others performing similar duties.

2. **C.** No filing fee is necessary, nor is it required that the successor firm even be in existence at the time of filing. The registration is effective for the unexpired portion of the year and then must be renewed (with a renewal fee) each December 31.

3. **A.** Under the Uniform Securities Act, a state registered investment adviser is required to meet the net worth and recordkeeping requirements of the state in which its principal office is located regardless of the requirements of any other state where it is also registered.

Quick Quiz 1.H

1. **F.** A consent to service of process is filed with the initial application and permanently remains on file with the Administrator.

2. **F.** There are no financial requirements for an investment adviser representative. Investment adviser representatives may be required to post a bond if they maintain discretion. Although the proper term for an investment adviser's requirement is net worth, the exam sometimes uses the term net capital instead.

3. **F.** A list of other states in which a securities professional intends to register is not required on a state application for registration.

2

Regulations of Securities and Issuers

State securities Administrators regulate securities transactions that occur in their states similarly to the way they regulate persons engaged in those transactions. This Unit discusses the procedures for the registration of securities as well as their exemptions from registration. For a securities transaction to be lawful under the USA, the security itself must be registered unless it or the transaction is exempt from registration requirements.

The Series 63 exam will include 6 questions on the material presented in this Unit. ■

When you have completed this Unit, you should be able to:

- **recognize** what is and what is not a security;

- **determine** who is and is not a security issuer;

- **compare** and contrast the different methods of securities registration;

- **identify** instruments that are securities;

- **list** the categories of exempt securities;

- **define** an exempt transaction and provide examples; and

- **describe** the requirements for exemption from registration for private placements.

2. 1 WHAT IS A SECURITY UNDER THE UNIFORM SECURITIES ACT?

Perhaps the most important term in the USA is the term *security*. Why is it so important? The reason is simple: the USA applies only to financial instruments that are securities. The purchase, sale, or issuance of anything that is not a security is not covered by the act. The definition of a security, however, is complex. Over the years, courts have determined case by case what constitutes a security. The US Supreme Court, in the Howey decision, defined the primary characteristics of what constitutes a security. For an instrument to be a security, the court held, it must constitute (1) an investment of money, (2) in a common enterprise, (3) with the expectation of profits, (4) to be derived primarily from the efforts of a person other than the investor. A **common enterprise** means an enterprise in which the fortunes of the investor are interwoven with those of either the person offering the investment, a third party, or other investors.

EXAMPLE

Let's show how common stock in a corporation meets the Howey definition. If you purchase shares, you have invested money (1); as have a number of other investors (2); hoping to make money by receiving dividends and/or selling the stock at a profit (3); and your success depends not on your efforts, but on the skill of the management of that corporation (4).

2. 1. 1 LIST OF SECURITIES UNDER THE UNIFORM SECURITIES ACT

The USA does not define the term *securities* but provides a comprehensive list of financial instruments that are securities under the act and therefore covered by its provisions. Under the USA, securities include:

- notes;
- stocks;
- treasury stocks;
- bonds;
- debentures;
- evidence of indebtedness;
- certificates of interest or participation in a profit-sharing agreement;
- collateral trust certificates;
- preorganization certificates or subscriptions;
- transferable shares;
- investment contracts;
- voting trust certificates;
- certificates of deposit for a security (ADRs, not a bank CD);
- fractional undivided interests in oil, gas, or other mineral rights;
- puts, calls, straddles, options, or privileges on a security;
- certificates of deposit or groups or indexes of securities;

- puts, calls, straddles, options, or privileges entered into on a national securities exchange relating to foreign currency;
- any interest or instrument commonly known as a security; or
- certificates of interest or participation in, receipts of, guarantees of, or warrants or rights to subscribe to or purchase, any of the above.

The following six items are not securities under the act:

- An insurance or endowment policy or annuity contract under which an insurance company promises to pay a fixed sum of money either in a lump sum or periodically
- Interest in a retirement plan, such as an IRA or Keogh plan
- Collectibles
- Commodities such as precious metals and grains or futures contracts for commodities
- Condominiums used as personal residences
- Currency

TEST TOPIC ALERT   The exam will want you to know what is and what is not a security. We suggest that you concentrate on learning the six that are not securities because they are much easier to remember and you will still be able to answer the questions correctly. You might also have to know that a confirmation of a securities trade is not a security; it is just a document evidencing that a transaction took place.

2. 1. 1. 1   Nonsecurity Investments

Although collectibles, precious metals, grains, futures, real estate, and currencies can be attractive investments, they are not securities. Because these items are not securities, their sale is not regulated by state securities law. Furthermore, if a registered agent commits fraud in the sale of any of these items, he has not committed a violation of state securities law. He has violated the antifraud provisions of another act prohibiting fraudulent commercial transactions.

EXAMPLE   An individual farmer's direct ownership of a cow is not a security—it is just owner-ship of a cow. However, if the farmer makes an investment of money in a tradable interest in a herd of cattle on which he expects to earn a profit solely as the result of the breeder's efforts, he has purchased a security. In the same manner, if a condominium is purchased in a resort area with the goal of placing it into a rental pool and renting it out most of the year, and it is used only for personal vacation time, the condo is considered a security because there is a profit motive, typically reliant on the efforts of a third party—the rental agent. On the other hand, if you have chosen to live in a condominium as a personal residence, it is a home, not a security.

TAKE NOTE   Annuities with fixed payouts are not securities, but variable annuities are because they are dependent on the investment performance of securities within the annuity.

2. 1. 2   NONEXEMPT SECURITY

A nonexempt security is a security subject to the registration provisions mandated by the USA. **Exempt** means not subject to registration. If a security is not registered or is not exempt from registration, it cannot be sold in a state unless in an exempt transaction. As you will see, the sale of an unregistered nonexempt security is a prohibited practice under the USA and may subject an agent to both civil and criminal penalties.

TAKE NOTE   The methods of registration discussed in this Unit refer to nonexempt securities because if they were exempt, they would not have to register. For example, a registered nonexempt security is most likely a common stock properly registered for sale in a state.

2. 1. 3   ISSUER

An **issuer** is any person who issues (distributes) or proposes to issue a security. The most common issuers of securities are companies or governments (federal, state, and municipal governments and their agencies and subdivisions).

If an issuer is nonexempt, it must register its securities in the states where they will be sold under one of the registration methods described in the Unit.

EXAMPLE   ABC Shoe Co. (a retail chain store) issues shares to the public. Mr. Bixby (an investor) buys the shares through his agent, Mr. Thompson, at First Securities Corporation. ABC Shoe is the issuer; Mr. Bixby is the investor; First Securities is the broker/dealer; and Mr. Thompson is the registered representative, known under the USA as an agent.

2. 1. 3. 1   Issuer Transaction

An **issuer transaction** is one in which the proceeds of the sale go to the issuer. All newly issued securities are issuer transactions. In other words, when a company raises money by selling (issuing) securities to investors, the proceeds from the sale go to the company itself.

2. 1. 3. 1. 1   Initial or Primary Offering

An issuer transaction involving new securities is called a **primary offering**. If it is the first time an issuer distributes securities to the public, it is called an **initial public offering (IPO)**. Initial or primary offerings are issuer transactions because the issuer (the company) receives the proceeds from the investor investing in the company.

2. 1. 3. 2   Nonissuer Transaction

A **nonissuer transaction** is one in which the proceeds of the sale do not go, directly or indirectly, to the entity that originally offered the securities to the public. The most common example is everyday trading in the secondary markets such as the New York Stock Exchange or Nasdaq. In a nonissuer transaction, the proceeds of the sale go to the investor who sold the shares. Since the shares are not "new," we refer to this as secondary trading.

TAKE NOTE

If Mr. Bixby, an investor, sells 100 shares of stock he owns in ABC Shoe Co. (the securities issuer) on the New York Stock Exchange (NYSE), Mr. Bixby receives the proceeds from the sale, not ABC Shoes. This is a nonissuer transaction.

Nonissuer transactions are also referred to as **secondary transactions** or **transactions between investors**.

EXAMPLE

The first time that ABC Shoe Co. issued shares to the public, ABC Shoe engaged in an IPO, or a primary offering, because it received the proceeds from distributing its shares to the public. After ABC Shoe went public, transactions between its investors executed on exchanges through brokerage agents were secondary transactions in nonissuer securities.

QUICK QUIZ 2.A

1. Which list of instruments below is NOT composed of securities?

   A. Stock, treasury stock, rights, warrants, transferable shares
   B. Voting trust certificates, interests in oil and gas drilling programs
   C. Commodity futures contracts, fixed-payment life insurance contracts
   D. Commodity options contracts, interests in multilevel distributorship arrangements

2. The US Supreme Court defined an investment contract as having 4 components. Which of the following is NOT part of the 4-part test for an investment contract?

   A. An investment of money
   B. An expectation of profit
   C. Management activity by owner
   D. Solely from the efforts of others

3. Nonexempt securities

   A. need not be registered in the state in which they are sold
   B. always must be registered in the state in which they are sold
   C. need not be registered if sold in an exempt transaction
   D. need not be registered if sold in a nonexempt transaction

4. A nonissuer transaction is a transaction

   A. between 2 corporations in which one is issuing the stock and the other is purchasing
   B. in which the issuing corporation will not receive the proceeds from the transaction
   C. in which a mutual fund purchases a Treasury bond directly from the government
   D. in which the security must be registered

Quick Quiz answers can be found at the end of the Unit.

2. 2 REGISTRATION OF SECURITIES UNDER THE UNIFORM SECURITIES ACT

It is unlawful for any person to offer or sell any security in this state unless (1) it is registered under the Act; (2) the security or transaction is exempted from registration under the Act; or (3) it is a federal covered security. If the security or transaction is not exempt or is not a federal covered security as defined by the NSMIA, it must be registered in the state or it cannot be lawfully sold in the state.

2. 2. 1 NATIONAL SECURITIES MARKETS IMPROVEMENT ACT OF 1996 (NSMIA)

We introduced you to the NSMIA in the previous Unit. This law effectively divided the responsibility for regulating investment advisers between the states and the SEC by bifurcating (splitting in two) the regulation of investment advisers and creating the category of registration known as a federal covered adviser. Of importance to this Unit, the NSMIA also created the term **federal covered security**, a security that was exempt from registration on the state level.

A federal covered security is simply a security that has a federally imposed exemption from state regulation. Most securities sold today are federal covered securities.

2. 2. 1. 1 Categories of Federal Covered Securities

The major categories of federal covered securities (securities covered by federal securities laws) that cannot be regulated by state securities Administrators (except for violating antifraud provisions), include:

- securities listed on the New York Stock Exchange, the American Stock Exchange, the Chicago Stock Exchange, the Nasdaq Stock Market, and (not tested) several other US exchanges. In addition, any security equal in seniority (rights or warrants) or senior to these securities (bonds and preferred stock) is also considered federal covered;
- investment company securities registered under the Investment Company Act of 1940, such as
  - open-end management investment companies (mutual funds),
  - closed-end management investment companies,
  - unit investment trusts, and
  - face-amount certificates; and
- offers and sales of certain exempt securities, such as
  - any security issued or guaranteed by the United States or any bank regulated by the Federal Reserve Board;
  - securities offered by a municipal issuer, unless the issuer is located in the state in which the municipal securities are being offered; and
  - offers and sales of securities sold through certain exempt transactions, such as securities offered to qualified purchasers under Regulation D of the Securities Act of 1933 (private placements).

TAKE NOTE
Although investment company securities are federal covered securities, the USA allows states to impose filing fees on them under a process called notice filing, described below. Other federal covered securities are generally not required to notice file, but the Administrator reserves the right to request a filing from listed and Nasdaq securities.

Bonds issued by municipalities—for example, City of New York bonds due in 2020—are federal covered securities exempt from registration requirements in the states. However, there is an exception to the rule. States may require registration of municipal securities of their own states, but they may not require registration of municipal securities issued by other states. Why? Municipal securities of other states are federal covered securities exempt from state registration. Municipal securities issued in an Administrator's state are not federal covered securities; they are not covered by the exemption (states retain authority over the issue of the municipal securities by their own municipalities). Even though these municipal bonds are exempt securities under the USA, they are not included in the NSMIA definition of federal covered security. Yes, this is confusing, but just try to keep it simple as in the following example:

EXAMPLE
A bond issued by the city of Columbus, OH, is a federal covered security everywhere *but* in the state of Ohio. The effect of this is that no state regulator can enforce any of their rules against the bond. But, in the state of Ohio, even though the security is exempt under Ohio's securities laws, the Administrator *could* request that the issuer (the city) furnish certain details about the issue.

So, are all securities registered with the SEC federal covered? No! States can require the registration of the securities of public offerings by non-bank, non-government issuers whose issues are traded in uncovered marketplaces such as the *Pink Sheets* or the OTC Bulletin Board. There are thousands of these companies, all registered with the SEC, but not meeting the standard to be considered federal covered. Therefore, as we will soon learn, these issues must be registered with both the SEC and the states.

2. 2. 2 METHODS OF STATE REGISTRATION OF SECURITIES

The USA provides three methods for securities issuers to register their securities in a state. They are:

- notice filing;
- coordination; and
- qualification.

2. 2. 2. 1 Notice Filing

As previously mentioned, The National Securities Markets Improvement Act of 1996 (NSMIA) designated certain securities as "federal covered" and, therefore, removed from the jurisdiction of the state regulatory authorities. Although the states are preempted from requiring registration for federal covered securities, status as a federal covered security is not a preemption of the licensing or anti-fraud laws. Any person who sells a federal covered security must be licensed as a broker/dealer or agent (unless otherwise exempted) and must also comply with the anti-fraud provisions of state laws.

The Uniform Securities Act gives the Administrator the authority to require notice filings with respect to federal covered securities, generally investment companies registered with the SEC under the Investment Company Act of 1940. So, what is this notice filing? Primarily, it is an opportunity for the states to collect revenue in the form of filing fees because, unlike with the other methods of registration we are going to discuss, the Administrator has limited powers to review any documentation filed with his department.

There is one category of federal covered security that is always required to engage in a special form of state registration known as Notice Filing. Investment companies must file a notice with the Administrator and will be required to pay the specified fees. These fees are generally lower than for the other forms of state registration.

Under the notice filing procedure, state Administrators may require the issuer to file the following documents as a condition for sale of their securities in the state:

■ Documents filed along with their registration statements filed with the SEC

■ Documents filed as amendments to the initial federal registration statement

■ A report on the value of such securities offered in the state

■ Consent to service of process

TEST TOPIC ALERT   Keep in mind the distinction between federal covered securities and SEC-registered securities. Under the NSMIA, federal covered securities are a narrowly defined group of securities that either trade on certain exchanges or are exempt from SEC registration. There are thousands of SEC-registered securities that do not meet the required standard, including those on the OTC Bulletin Board and the *Pink Sheets*.

TEST TOPIC ALERT   Before the initial offer of any federal covered security in this state, the Administrator may, by rule or order, require the filing of all documents that are part of a federal registration statement filed with the US Securities and Exchange Commission under the Securities Act of 1933, together with a consent to service of process signed by the issuer.

TEST TOPIC ALERT   Even though an issuer of a federal covered security (think about a Fortune 500 company listed on the NYSE) may not have to notice file, that does not mean that the company can make misrepresentations during an offer made in any state. To do so would violate the anti-fraud provisions of the USA.

2.2.2.2   Registration by Coordination

A security may be registered by coordination if a registration statement has been filed under the Securities Act of 1933 in connection with the same offering.

In coordinating a federal registration with state registration, issuers must supply the following records in addition to the consent to service of process:

■ Copies of the latest form of prospectus filed under the Securities Act of 1933 if the Administrator requires

- Copy of articles of incorporation and bylaws, a copy of the underwriting agreement, or a specimen copy of the security
- If the Administration requests, copies of any other information filed by the issuer under the Securities Act of 1933
- Each amendment to the federal prospectus promptly after it is filed with the SEC

2. 2. 2. 2. 1   Effective Date

Registration by coordination becomes effective at the same time the federal registration becomes effective, provided:

- no stop orders have been issued by the Administrator and no proceedings are pending against the issuer;
- the registration has been on file for at least the minimum number of days specified by the Administrator, a number that currently ranges from 10 to 20 days, depending on the state; and
- a statement of the maximum and minimum proposed offering prices and maximum underwriting discounts and commissions have been on file for two full business days.

Registration by coordination is by far the most frequently used method and, from a practical standpoint, is the only sensible way to register a multi-state offering.

2. 2. 2. 3   Registration by Qualification

Any security can be registered by qualification. Registration by qualification requires a registrant to supply any information required by the state securities Administrator. Securities not eligible for registration by another method must be registered by qualification. In addition, securities that will be sold only in one state (intrastate) will be registered by qualification.

To register by qualification, an issuer must supply a consent to service of process and the following information:

- Name, address, and form of organization; description of property; and nature of business
- Information on directors and officers and every owner of 10% or more of the issuer's securities, and the remuneration paid to owners in the last 12 months
- Description of the issuer's capitalization and long-term debt
- Estimated proceeds and the use to which the proceeds will be put
- Type and amount of securities offered, offering price, and selling and underwriting costs
- Stock options to be created in connection with the offering
- Copy of any prospectus, pamphlet, circular, or sales literature to be used in the offering
- Specimen copy of the security along with opinion of counsel as to the legality of the security being offered
- Audited balance sheet current within four months of the offering with an income statement for three years before the balance sheet date

The Administrator may require additional information by rule or order. The Administrator may require that a prospectus be sent to purchasers before the sale and that newly established companies register their securities for the first time in a state by qualification.

TAKE NOTE

As we've noted previously, in order to register, even by notice filing, there must be a consent to service of process filed with the Administrator. However, a person (remember the broad definition) who has filed such a consent in connection with a previous registration or notice filing need not file another. A practical effect of this is if you leave the firm you are registering with (you've probably already filed the consent to service of process to get this far) and register with another firm, you do not have to file a new consent—the old one remains on file. Or, if a company decides to raise additional capital by issuing more stock, a new consent is not required.

2. 2. 2. 3. 1   *Effective Date*

Unlike coordination, in which the effective date is triggered by SEC acceptance of the registration, a registration by qualification becomes effective whenever the state Administrator so orders.

Regardless of the method used, every registration statement is effective for one year from its effective date. Unlike agent and broker/dealer registrations, the date December 31 is of no consequence. One interesting facet of the law is that the registration may remain in effect past the first anniversary if there are still some unsold shares remaining, as long as they are still being offered at the original public offering price by either the issuer or the underwriter.

Although the previous rule applies to all methods of registration, as a practical matter, it would rarely apply other than in a security registered by Qualification. Those registered by Coordination are also obviously registered with the SEC and therefore are sold by the major investment banking houses. Unless the issue is a real dog, it will sell out rather quickly. Even those that are not popular are usually completely subscribed to in a week or two.

On the other hand, what if the issue, regardless of the method of registration, is in very high demand? Is it possible to increase the number of shares in the offering without having to file a new registration statement? Yes. A registration statement may be amended after its effective date so as to increase the securities specified to be offered and sold if two conditions are met: (1) the public offering price and (2) the underwriters' discounts and commissions are not changed from the respective amounts stated in the original registration statement.

The amendment becomes effective when the Administrator so orders. Every person filing such an amendment shall pay a late registration fee and a filing fee, calculated in the manner as the original quantity, levied against the additional securities proposed to be offered.

TEST TOPIC ALERT

A registration statement may be amended after its effective date to change the number of shares to be offered and sold if the public offering price and underwriter's discounts and commissions are unchanged.

QUICK QUIZ 2.B

True or False?

_____ 1. ABC Shoe Company, a new retail shoe store chain, has applied for the registration of its securities with the SEC as required by the Securities Act of 1933 and wants to register its securities in the state of Illinois. ABC Shoe Company would most likely register by coordination.

_____ 2. Any company may register by qualification whether or not it files a statement with the SEC.

2. 3   EXEMPTIONS FROM REGISTRATION

In certain situations, the USA exempts both securities and transactions from registration and filing requirements of sales literature. A security, a transaction, or both, can be exempt.

An **exempt security** retains its exemption when initially issued and in subsequent trading. However, justification as an **exempt transaction** must be established before each transaction.

The USA provides for a number of categories of exempt securities and even more categories of exempt transactions. Those securities that are **nonexempt** must register unless sold in exempt transactions. As mentioned above, an **exempt security** retains its exemption at its initial issue and in subsequent trading.

An exemption for a transaction, on the other hand, must be established with each transaction. Provided it is in the public interest, the state Administrator can deny, suspend, or revoke any securities transaction exemption other than that of a federal covered security. This action may be taken with or without prior notice (summarily).

TAKE NOTE   A security is exempt because of the nature of the issuer, not the purchaser.

An **exempt transaction** is exempt from the regulatory control of the state Administrator because of the manner in which a sale is made or because of the person to whom the sale is made. A transaction is an action and must be judged by the merits of each instance.

One of the most important statements found in the USA is the following.

It is unlawful for any person to offer or sell any security in this state unless:

- it is registered under the act;
- the security or transaction is exempted under the act; or
- it is a federal covered security.

For example, an agent can sell a security that is not exempt from registration in the state if the purchaser of the security is a bank or other institutional buyer. Why is that so? Because the sale of securities to certain financial institutions is an exempt transaction (as will be enumerated shortly), the sale can be made without registration. This means that the securities sold in exempt transactions do not have to be registered in the state. If such securities were not sold in exempt transactions, such as to an individual investor, they would have to be registered in the state.

2. 3. 1   EXEMPT SECURITIES

Securities exempt from state registration are also exempt from state filing of sales literature. Exempt securities include the following.

- **US and Canadian government and municipal securities**. These include securities issued, insured, or guaranteed by the United States or Canada, by a state or province, or by their political subdivisions.
- **Foreign government securities**. These include securities issued, insured, or guaranteed by a foreign government with which the United States maintains diplomatic relations.
- **Depository institutions**. These include securities that are issued, guaranteed by, or a direct obligation of a depository institution (depository institution means any bank, savings institution, or trust company organized and supervised under the laws of the United

States or any state). Securities issued by a savings and loan association are exempt only if the institution is authorized to do business in the state.

■ **Insurance company securities.** These include securities issued, insured, or guaranteed by an insurance company authorized to do business in the state. Insurance company securities refer to the stocks or bonds issued by insurance companies, not the variable policies sold by the companies. Fixed insurance and annuity policies are not securities.

■ **Public utility securities.** These include any security issued or guaranteed by a public utility or public utility holding company, or an equipment trust certificate issued by a railroad or other common carrier regulated in respect to rates by federal or state authority; or regulated in respect to issuance or guarantee of the security by a governmental authority of the United States, any state, Canada, or any Canadian province.

■ **Federal covered securities.** These include any security of an issuer equal to or senior to the common stock, such as include rights, warrants, preferred stock, and any debt security.

■ **Securities issued by nonprofit organizations.** These include securities issued by religious, educational, fraternal, charitable, social, athletic, reformatory, or trade associations. Nonprofit is the key word.

■ **Securities issued by cooperatives.** These include securities issued by a nonprofit membership cooperative to members of that cooperative.

■ **Securities of employee benefit plans.** These include any investment contract issued by an employee stock purchase, saving, pension, or profit-sharing plan.

■ **Certain money market instruments.** Commercial paper and banker's acceptances are the two most common examples.

The distinction between exemptions and exceptions (or exclusions) from definitions is important in view of the fact that an exempt security is not exempt from the anti-fraud provisions of the Uniform Securities Act.

For example, as we covered earlier in this Unit, the typical life insurance policy or fixed annuity is not a "security," and the blue sky law has no impact on it. On the other hand, we have just seen that securities issued by insurance companies are exempted from registration under the conditions of the Act. Even though these securities are exempt from registration and the filing of advertising and sales literature with the Administrator, they are still subject to the anti-fraud provisions. Therefore, one cannot be charged with fraudulent behavior in the sale of a fixed annuity while one could be with the sale of stock in an insurance company (or any other exempt security).

TAKE NOTE

A promissory note (commercial paper), draft, bill of exchange, or banker's acceptance that matures within nine months, is issued in denominations of at least $50,000, and receives one of the three highest ratings by a nationally recognized rating agency is a federal covered security and also is exempt from registration requirements. Please note that this is the only case where a security's rating is part of the registration or exemption under the Uniform Securities Act.

QUICK QUIZ 2.C

1. Which of the following securities is(are) exempt from the registration and advertising filing requirements under the USA?

    I. Shares of investment companies registered under the Investment Company Act of 1940
    II. Shares sold on the Nasdaq Stock Market
    III. AAA rated promissory notes of $100,000 that mature in 30 days
    IV. Shares sold on the New York Stock Exchange

    A. I only
    B. II, III and IV
    C. II and IV
    D. I, II, III and IV

2. Which of the following securities is NOT exempt from the registration and advertising requirements of the USA?

    A. Shares of Commonwealth Edison, a regulated public utility holding company
    B. Securities issued by the Carnegie Endowment for Peace
    C. Securities issued by a bank that is a member of the Federal Reserve System
    D. Variable annuity contract issued by Metrodential Insurance Co.

2.3.2   EXEMPT TRANSACTIONS

Before a security can be sold in a state, it must be registered unless exempt from registration or traded in an exempt transaction. This section covers exemptions for transactions that take place in a state.

There are many different types of exempt transactions. We begin by focusing on those most likely to be on your exam and finish with several others.

- **Isolated nonissuer transactions.** Isolated nonissuer transactions include secondary (nonissuer) transactions, whether effected through a broker/dealer or not, that occur infrequently (very few transactions per agent per year; the exact number varies by state). However, these usually do not involve securities professionals. In the same manner that individuals placing a "for sale by owner" sign on their front lawns do not need a real estate license, one individual selling stock to another in a one-on-one transaction is engaging in a transaction exempt from the oversight of the Administrator because the issuer is not receiving any of the proceeds and the parties involved are not trading as part of a regular practice.

- **Unsolicited brokerage transactions.** These include transactions initiated by the client, not the agent. They are the most common of the exempt transactions. If a client calls a registered agent and requests that the agent buy or sell a security, the transaction is an unsolicited brokerage transaction exempt from state registration. But, the Administrator may by rule require that the customer acknowledge upon a specified form that the sale was unsolicited and that a signed copy of the form be kept by the broker/dealer for a specified period.

- **Underwriter transactions.** These include transactions between issuer and underwriter (such as a firm commitment underwriting) as well as those between underwriters themselves (as when functioning as members of a selling syndicate).

- **Bankruptcy, guardian, or conservator transactions.** Transactions by an executor, administrator, marshal, sheriff, trustee in bankruptcy, or other fiduciary are exempt transactions.

TEST TOPIC ALERT   Note that a custodian under UTMA or UGMA is not included in this list and that the only trustee who is included is one in a bankruptcy case.

- **Institutional investor transactions**. These are primarily transactions with financial institutions such as banks, insurance companies, and investment companies. Employee benefit plans with assets of at least $1 million are also included. There is no minimum order size used to determine these trades.

- **Limited offering transactions**. These include any offering, called a private placement, directed at not more than 10 persons (called **offerees**) other than institutional investors during the previous 12 consecutive months, provided that:

  — the seller reasonably believes that all of the noninstitutional buyers are purchasing for investment purposes only;

  — no commissions or other remuneration is paid for soliciting noninstitutional investors; and

  — no general solicitation or advertising is used.

  Unlike federal law, where the private placement rule restricts the number of purchasers, the USA restricts the number of offers that may be made.

  There is another way in which the USA differs from the federal law on private placements. The federal law will *not* be tested, but we are referring to it because we know many of our Series 63 students have just completed studying for a FINRA exam where this topic is covered, and we don't want you to choose the wrong answer on this test. Under federal law, any non-institutional purchaser must sign an *investment letter* indicating that purchase was made for investment purposes only and not for immediate resale. However, the USA does not require a written representation by each buyer that he is purchasing for investment, but agrees that it would be prudent on the part of the seller to obtain something in writing. All that is required is that the seller *reasonably* believes that the buyer is purchasing for investment only. Moreover, one who in good faith buys for investment can later change his mind and resell, although the shorter the interval, the harder it will be to show that there was a bona fide change of mind.

  The number 10 is the figure that will be tested. But, an Administrator may want to reduce it, for example, for uranium stocks or oil royalties, or increase it for a closely-held corporation that wants to solicit 20 or 30 friends and relatives of the owners for additional capital. As we continue to learn, the Administrator has a great deal of power.

- **Preorganization certificates**. An offer or sale of a preorganization certificate or subscription is exempt if:

  — no commission or other remuneration is paid or given directly or indirectly for soliciting any subscriber;

  — the number of subscribers does not exceed 10; and

  — no payment is made by any subscriber.

  You have probably never heard of a preorganization certificate or subscription, so a little explanation is in order. A new corporation cannot receive a charter unless their documents of incorporation provide evidence that minimum funding is assured. Since the purpose of these preorganization certificates is to enable a new enterprise to obtain the minimum number of subscriptions required by the corporation law, the USA places a limitation on the number of *subscribers* rather than the number of offerees (as in the private placement exemption above). Hence, there may be a publicly advertised offering of preorganization subscriptions. But there may be *no payment* until effective registration unless another exemption is available. This tool itself simply postpones registration; it does not excuse registration altogether.

■ **Transactions with existing security holders**. A transaction made under an offer to existing security holders of the issuer (including persons who are holders of convertible securities, rights, or warrants) is exempt as long as no commission or other form of remuneration is paid directly or indirectly for soliciting that security holder.

■ **Nonissuer transactions by pledgees**. A nonissuer transaction executed by a bona fide pledgee (i.e., the one who received the security as collateral for a loan), as long as it was not for the purpose of evading the act, is an exempt transaction. For example, you pledged stock as collateral for a loan and defaulted on your obligation. The lender will sell your stock to try to recoup his loss and, under the USA, this is considered an exempt transaction.

The following are examples of exempt transactions that are unlikely to be on your exam.

■ **Unit secured transactions**. These include transactions in a bond backed by a real mortgage or deed of trust provided that the entire mortgage or deed of trust is sold as a unit.

■ **Control transactions**. This includes mergers, consolidations, or reorganization transactions to which the issuer and the other person or its parent or subsidiary are parties.

■ **Rescission offers**. These include offers made to rescind an improper transaction.

TAKE NOTE

Some students find it helpful to remember that an exempt security is a noun while an exempt transaction is a verb (hence the word *action*).

TEST TOPIC ALERT

Remember the distinction between an accredited investor and institutional investor. An **accredited investor** is an investor who meets the accredited investor standards of Regulation D. Regulation D standards require that an individual have a net worth (exclusive of the net equity in a primary residence) greater than $1 million or $200,000 in income for the last two years and the current year, invest for his own account, and have requisite knowledge to evaluate investments. This term only applies to federal law, not the USA, and probably will never be the correct answer to a USA question.

An **institutional investor** is an investor that manages large amounts of money, such as a mutual fund, an insurance company, a bank, or a pension fund.

2. 3. 3 ADMINISTRATOR'S POWER OVER EXEMPTIONS

The USA grants the Administrator the authority, by rule or order, to exempt a security, transaction, or offer from the USA's registration and filing requirements. In addition, the Administrator may waive a requirement for an exemption of a transaction or security.

Try to follow this next point because it is a bit tricky. The Administrator may, by rule or order, deny or revoke the registration exemption of:

■ any security issued by any person organized and operated not for private profit but exclusively for religious, educational, benevolent, charitable, fraternal, social, athletic, or reformatory purposes, or as a chamber of commerce or trade or professional association (your basic nonprofit exemption); and

■ any investment contract issued in connection with an employees' stock purchase, savings, pension, profit sharing, or similar benefit plan.

Please note that a few pages ago, we gave you a list of 10 different exempt securities, from US and Canadian government issues through certain money market instruments. However, the Administrator can only deny exemption to the two specified above. On the other hand, with the exception of those involving federal covered securities, the Administrator may deny any exempt transaction. That means that, for example, just because an agent solicited a transaction with an insurance company of a security that was not federal covered, the Administrator has the power, if he feels it is justified, to consider that transaction nonexempt.

Under the USA, the burden of providing an exemption or an exception from a definition falls upon the person claiming it. If the aggrieved party wishes to contest the Administrator's removal of an exemption, the Administrator must provide an opportunity for a hearing within *15 days* of the receipt of a written request.

TAKE NOTE   There are only two securities exemptions that the Administrator may revoke, whereas all exempt transactions, other than in federal covered securities, may be revoked.

2. 3. 4   SUMMARY OF EXEMPTIONS FROM REGISTRATION

Let's start our summary with the key statement from the USA:

> It is unlawful for any person to offer or sell any security in this state unless (1) it is registered under this act or (2) the security or transaction is exempted under this act; or (3) it is a federal covered security.

We must point out that these exemptions apply to the security or transaction only, not to the securities professional. So if a security is exempt, such as a government security, it can be sold in this state without any registration. But, the person who sells it must be properly registered in this state (unless that person qualifies for an exemption). Are you confused? Remember, we learned in Unit 1 that broker/dealers with no place of business in the state, dealing exclusively with other broker/dealers or institutional clients, are not considered to be a B/D in the state (as long as they are properly registered in at least one state—the location of their principal office). Let's apply that to the following situation.

ABC Securities is a broker/dealer registered in State A. They have no place of business in State B, but they do effect transactions on behalf of a number of banks and insurance companies located in State B. Therefore, they are not considered B/Ds in State B and are exempt from registering. Should ABC Securities sell some government securities to these clients, neither ABC nor the agents making the sale are required to be registered. This is not because the government securities are exempt (that just means that *they* don't have to register with the Administrator), but because, under the USA, ABC does not meet the definition of a broker/dealer in State B.

However, should ABC decide to have any of their agents sell these government bonds to individual (sometimes referred to as *retail*) clients in State B, then, even though the bonds are exempt securities, both ABC and the selling agents must register in that state.

The same applies to exempt transactions. One of the most common cases is when a client calls an agent to purchase a security that is not exempt and not registered in your state. But, because the transaction has been initiated by the client, as an unsolicited trade, it is an exempt transaction and, therefore, the trade may be made even though the security is not registered.

One way the exam will try to trick you is by asking about an individual calling a agent from a state in which the agent is not registered. The broker/dealer is registered in that state, and the individual is a client of the firm, but not that particular agent. The individual wishes to enter an unsolicited order—can the agent accept it? No! Although the transaction is exempt (which only means that the security does not have to be registered in that state), an agent can only do business with a resident of a state if the agent is properly licensed in that state. In this case, the agent would have to turn the order over to an agent who is licensed in that other state.

QUICK QUIZ 2.D

Indicate an exempt transaction with **Y** and a nonexempt transaction with **N**.

_____ 1. Mr. Thompson, an agent with First Securities, Inc. (a broker/dealer), receives an unsolicited request to purchase a security for Mary Gordon, a high net worth individual

_____ 2. The sale of an unregistered security in a private, nonpublicly advertised transaction offered to 10 or fewer investors over the last 12 months

_____ 3. The sale of unclaimed securities by the sheriff of Santa Fe, New Mexico

_____ 4. Sale of stock of a privately owned company to the public in an initial public offering

5. Which of the following are exempt transactions?

   I.   An agent sells a security issued by a foreign government with which the United States has diplomatic relations to an individual client
   II. An unsolicited request from an existing client to purchase a nonexempt security
   III. The sale of an unregistered security in a private, nonpublicly advertised transaction to 14 noninstitutional investors over a period not exceeding 12 months
   IV. The sale of unlisted securities by a trustee in bankruptcy

   A. I and II
   B. I and III
   C. II and IV
   D. III and IV

---

2. 4 STATE SECURITIES REGISTRATION PROCEDURES

The first step in the registration procedure is for the issuer or its representative to complete a registration application and file it with the state securities Administrator. The person registering the securities is known as the **registrant**.

2. 4. 1   FILING THE REGISTRATION STATEMENT

State Administrators require every issuer to supply the following information on their applications:

- Amount of securities to be issued in the state
- States in which the security is to be offered, but not the amounts offered in those other states
- Any adverse order or judgment concerning the offering by regulatory authorities, court, or the SEC
- Anticipated effective date
- Anticipated use of the proceeds (why are we raising this money?)

When filing the registration statement with the Administrator, an applicant may include documents that have been filed with the Administrator within the last five years, provided the information is current and accurate. The Administrator may, by rule or order, permit the omission of any information it considers unnecessary.

TEST TOPIC ALERT   One item that will not be found in the registration statement is the rating of the security.

TEST TOPIC ALERT   Although most registration statements are filed by the issuer, the exam may require you to know that they may also be filed by any selling stockholder, such as an insider making a large block sale, or by a broker/dealer.

2. 4. 2   FILING FEE

The issuer (or any other person on whose behalf the offering is to be made) must pay a filing fee as determined by the Administrator when filing the registration. The filing fees are often based on a percentage of the total offering price.

If the registration is withdrawn or if the Administrator issues a stop order before the registration is effective, the Administrator may retain a portion of the fee and refund the remainder to the applicant.

2. 4. 3   ONGOING REPORTS

The Administrator may require the person who filed the registration statement to file reports to keep the information contained in the registration statement current and to inform the Administrator of the progress of the offering.

TAKE NOTE   These reports cannot be required more often than quarterly.

2. 4. 4   ESCROW

As a condition of registration under coordination or qualification, the Administrator may require that a security be placed in **escrow** if the security is issued:

■ within the past three years;

■ to a promoter at a price substantially different than the offering price; or

■ to any person for a consideration other than cash.

In addition, the Administrator may require that the proceeds from the sale of the registered security in this state be impounded until the issuer receives a specified amount from the sale of the security either in this state or elsewhere. There have been many instances where companies were unable to raise their targeted goal and just took the money and ran. This impound, or escrow, lessens the likelihood that this will happen.

2. 4. 5   SPECIAL SUBSCRIPTION FORM

The Administrator may also require, as a condition of registration, that the issue be sold only on a form specified by the Administrator and that a copy of the form or subscription contract be filed with the Administrator or preserved for up to three years.

TAKE NOTE

A registration statement may not be withdrawn by a registrant until one year after its effective date if any securities of the same class are outstanding and may only be withdrawn with the approval of the Administrator.

QUICK QUIZ 2.E

1. With regard to the registration requirements of the Uniform Securities Act, which of the following statements are TRUE?

   I.   Only the issuer itself can file a registration statement with the Administrator.
   II. An application for registration must indicate the amount of securities to be issued in the state.
   III. The Administrator may require registrants to file quarterly reports.

   A. I and II
   B. I and III
   C. II and III
   D. I, II and III

---

2. 4. 6   PROSPECTUS DELIVERY REQUIREMENTS

As previously mentioned, the Administrator may require that, in the case of a security registered by qualification, the prospectus be delivered prior to or concurrent with the sale. For registrants using the other methods, the USA follows the rules of the Securities Act of 1933 requiring that delivery be no later than the mailing of the trade confirmation or actual delivery of the security.

TAKE NOTE

In the next Unit, we will learn what the Administrator can do to deny a registration so that it does not become effective or, when it has already become effective, to suspend or revoke the registration.

UNIT TEST

1. Which of the following is defined as a security under the Uniform Securities Act?

    A. A guaranteed, lump-sum payment to a beneficiary
    B. Fixed, guaranteed payments made for life or for a specified period
    C. Commodity futures contracts
    D. An investment contract

2. Under the Uniform Securities Act, which of the following persons is responsible for proving that a securities issue is exempt from registration?

    A. Underwriter
    B. Issuer
    C. State Administrator
    D. There is no need to prove eligibility for an exemption

3. Registration is effective when ordered by the Administrator in the case of registration by

    A. coordination
    B. integration
    C. notice filing
    D. qualification

4. The US Supreme Court in the Howey decision ruled that an instrument that represents the investment of money in a common enterprise with an expectation of profit solely through the managerial efforts of others is a security. According to the Howey decision, the USA would consider which of the following a security?

    A. Purchase of a house in a desirable real estate market with the expectation that the house will be resold at a profit within a few years
    B. Purchase of jewelry for speculative purposes as opposed to personal use
    C. Investment in options to acquire a security
    D. Investment in commodities futures

5. Under the Uniform Securities Act, which of the following would be considered an exempt transaction?

    I. An existing client calls to purchase 1,000 shares of a common stock that is not registered in this state
    II. The sale to an individual client of shares that are part of a registered secondary of a NYSE-listed company
    III. The sale of shares of a bank's IPO to an institutional client
    IV. The sale of shares of an insurance company's IPO to an individual client

    A. I and III
    B. I, III and IV
    C. II and IV
    D. I, II, III and IV

6. Which of the following securities is(are) exempt from the registration provisions of the USA?

    I. Common stock issued by a savings and loan association authorized to do business in the state
    II. General obligation municipal bond
    III. Bond issued by a company that has common stock listed on the American Stock Exchange

    A. I only
    B. II only
    C. II and III
    D. I, II and III

7. A primary transaction is

    A. the first transaction between two parties in the over-the-counter market
    B. a sale between investors of securities traded on the New York Stock Exchange
    C. a new offering of an issuer sold to investors
    D. a secondary market transaction in a security recently offered to the public

8. All of the following describe exempt transactions EXCEPT

    A. ABC, a broker/dealer, purchases securities from XYZ Corporation

    B. First National Bank sells its entire publicly traded bond portfolio to Amalgamated National Bank

    C. Amalgamated National Bank sells its publicly traded bond portfolio to ABC Insurance Company

    D. Joe Smith, an employee of Amalgamated Bank, buys securities from ABC Brokerage Corporation

9. Under the USA, all of the following are exempt securities EXCEPT

    I. US government securities

    II. unsolicited transactions

    III. transactions between issuers and underwriters

    IV. securities of credit unions

    A. I, II and IV

    B. I and IV

    C. II and III

    D. IV only

10. Registration statements for securities under the Uniform Securities Act are effective for

    A. a period determined by the Administrator for each issue

    B. 1 year from the effective date

    C. 1 year from the date of issue

    D. 1 year from the previous January 1

11. Under the Uniform Securities Act, an issuer is any person who issues, or proposes to issue, a security for sale to the public. According to the USA, which of the following is(are) NOT an issuer?

    I. The City of Chicago, which is involved in a distribution of tax-exempt highway improvement bonds

    II. A partner in the AAA Oil and Gas Partnership, who sells his interest in the investment

    III. The AAA Manufacturing Company, which proposes to offer shares to the public but has not completed the offering

    IV. The US government, which proposes to offer Treasury bonds

    A. I only

    B. II only

    C. I, II and III

    D. I, II and IV

12. Which of the following would be considered exempt transactions under the USA?

    I. A trustee of a corporation in bankruptcy liquidates securities to satisfy debt holders

    II. An offer of a securities investment is directed to 10 individuals in the state during a 12-month consecutive period

    III. An agent frequently engages in nonissuer transactions in unregistered securities in his own account

    IV. Agents for an entrepreneur offer preorganization certificates to fewer than 10 investors in the state for a modest commission

    A. I and II

    B. I, III and IV

    C. I and IV

    D. II and IV

13. Which of the following is(are) primary transactions?

    I. John inherited securities of XYZ Corporation from his father who, as a founder of the company, received the shares directly from the company as a result of stock options.
    II. John sold the securities he had inherited from his father to his neighbor, Peter, at the market price without charging a commission.
    III. John's father, a founder of XYZ Corporation, purchased shares of XYZ directly from the corporation after its founding without paying a commission.
    IV. John purchased shares in XYZ Corporation in a third-market transaction.

    A. I only
    B. I and II
    C. III only
    D. I, II, III and IV

14. XYZ Corporation has been in business for over 20 years. It needs additional capital for expansion and determines that a public offering in its home state and neighboring states is appropriate. Which method of securities registration most likely would be used to register this initial public offering?

    A. Coordination
    B. Notice filing
    C. Qualification
    D. Any of the above

15. Which of the following meet the USA's definition of an exempt transaction?

    I. Transactions by an executor of an estate
    II. Transactions with an investment company registered under the Investment Company Act of 1940
    III. An unsolicited sale of a Bulletin Board stock
    IV. Sale of a new issue to an individual customer

    A. I and II
    B. I, II and III
    C. IV only
    D. I, II, III and IV

16. By order and with prompt notice, the Administrator could revoke the exemption of all of the following EXCEPT

    A. an Atlanta, Georgia, school district bond
    B. an unsolicited trade of a common stock traded on the Pink Sheets
    C. a security issued by a fraternal organization
    D. a sale made to a bank

17. Which of the following are exempt securities?

    I. Securities guaranteed by domestic banks
    II. Securities issued by the government of Canada
    III. Securities issued exclusively for religious purposes
    IV. Federal covered securities

    A. I, II and III
    B. II only
    C. II and IV
    D. I, II, III and IV

18. All of the following are exempt transactions EXCEPT

    A. transactions by a guardian
    B. sale of a registered IPO to an individual client
    C. unsolicited secondary market transactions
    D. transactions by a broker/dealer with a registered investment company

19. Most securities must be registered under state laws; however, certain securities are exempt under the act. One of the exemptions is the federal covered security, which covers

    I. any security listed on a major stock exchange
    II. all Nasdaq-listed securities
    III. securities meeting certain financial tests of liquidity and net worth
    IV. bank and insurance company securities

    A. I only
    B. I and II
    C. I, II and IV
    D. I and III

20. Under the Uniform Securities Act, the Administrator may require an agent to present the prospectus for a new issue to the offeree

    A. prior to making the offer
    B. prior to making the sale
    C. prior to the effective date of the issue
    D. once payment has been made

ANSWERS AND RATIONALES

1. **D.** Investment contracts are defined as securities under the Uniform Securities Act. In fact, the term is often used as a synonym for a security. A guaranteed, lump-sum payment to a beneficiary is an endowment policy excluded from the definition of a security. Fixed, guaranteed payments made for life or for a specified period are fixed annuity contracts not defined as securities. Commodity futures contracts and the commodities themselves are not securities. Remember, it is much easier to remember what is not a security than what is.

2. **B.** The burden of proof for claiming eligibility for an exemption falls to the person claiming the exemption. In the event the registration statement was filed by someone other than the issuer (such as a selling stockholder or broker/dealer), that person must prove the claim.

3. **D.** Registration by qualification is the only registration method in which the Administrator sets the effective date. The effective date under registration by coordination is set by the SEC, and notice filing is merely the filing of certain documents enabling the registrant to offer securities in that state.

4. **C.** The investment in options is the only choice that meets the definition of security. It is an investment in a common enterprise with the expectation that the owner will profit as a result of the managerial efforts of others. The purchase of a house or jewelry is a purchase of a real asset or product that may result in a profit for the owner but not as a result of the managerial efforts of a third party. Commodities futures contracts are specifically excluded from the definition of a security. Note that options on futures, however, are securities under the USA. Remember the items that are not securities.

5. **A.** A client calling to purchase stock is an unsolicited transaction, probably the most common of the exempt transactions. Any sale to an institutional client is an exempt transaction while those to individuals, unless unsolicited, generally are not. Please note that even though the NYSE listed stock (a federal covered security) is exempt, the transaction is not.

6. **D.** The USA exempts from registration a number of different issues, including securities issued by a bank or anything that resembles a bank (a savings and loan or a credit union). Securities issued by a governmental unit are always exempt. Securities listed on the American Stock Exchange are part of a group known as federal covered securities that also includes securities listed on the New York Stock Exchange and Nasdaq Stock Market issues.

7. **C.** A primary transaction is a new offering of securities by an issuer sold to investors. Transactions between two investors in the over-the-counter market are called secondary transactions (the market between investors). A sale between investors of securities traded on the New York Stock Exchange is another example of a secondary transaction.

8. **D.** The purchase of securities from a broker/dealer by an employee of a bank is a nonexempt transaction—it is a sale of a security by a broker/dealer to a member of the public and is therefore not exempt. Transactions between brokers and issuers, transactions between banks, and transactions between banks and insurance companies are exempt because they are transactions between financial institutions. Exempt transactions are most often identified by whom the transaction is with rather than by what type of security is involved.

9. **C.** Both unsolicited transactions and transactions between issuers and underwriters are exempt transactions, not exempt securities. US government securities and securities of credit unions are exempt securities, not exempt transactions.

10. **B.** Securities registration statements are effective for 1 year from the effective date.

11. **B.** Under the Uniform Securities Act, an issuer is any person who issues, or proposes to issue, a security. Examples of issuers are a municipality such as the city of Chicago, which issues tax-exempt highway improvement bonds; the AAA Manufacturing Company, which proposes to offer shares to the public even though it has not completed the offering; and the US government, when it proposes to offer Treasury bonds. Oil, gas, and mining partnerships are not issuers under the terms of the Uniform Securities Act; however, certificates of interest in them are securities. The resale of a partnership interest by an investor is a nonissuer sale because the investor is not the issuer.

12. **A.** Transactions by fiduciaries, such as a trustee in a bankruptcy reorganization, are exempt from registration. An offer of a securities investment to 10 or fewer individuals (called a private placement) is also exempt from registration. Engaging in nonissuer transactions on a regular basis is not exempt from registration. That exemption is granted only in the case of isolated transactions, the opposite of regular. Offers of preorganization certificates are not exempt when commissions are charged.

13. **C.** A primary transaction is one in which the issuer of the securities receives the proceeds of the sale. John's father, although a founder of the company, purchased shares directly from the company. This transaction is a primary transaction because the firm received the funds from the sale of the shares. In all the other instances, the firm, the original issuer of the securities, did not receive the proceeds of the transaction. These transactions are called nonissuer transactions.

14. **A.** Because this offering is being made in more than one state, SEC registration is necessary; the state registration method would be coordination, which is the simultaneous registration of a security with both the SEC and the states.

15. **B.** Transactions by a fiduciary, such as the executor of an estate, are included in the definition of exempt transaction, as well as transactions with certain institutional clients, such as investment companies and insurance companies. The OTC Bulletin Board is an electronic medium for the trading of highly speculative, thinly capitalized issues. Because the order is an unsolicited one, the transaction is exempt. Sale of a new issue of stock to an individual client would not be an exempt transaction.

16. **A.** Certain security exemptions may never be revoked by the Administrator. Most important among these exemptions are governments, municipals, insurance companies, and banks. The Administrator can revoke the exemption of a security issued by a specific nonprofit entity. The Administrator can also revoke the exemption of any exempt transaction except one involving a federal covered security. A Pink Sheet stock is *not* federal covered. Remember the difference between an exempt security and an exempt transaction. Whether the security is exempt depends on who the issuer is. Whether the transaction is exempt depends on whom the trade is with or how the trade is made.

17. **D.** Among the exempt securities under the Uniform Securities Act (meaning exempt from the registration requirements) are securities issued by banks, securities issued by a recognized foreign government (particularly Canadian securities), securities issued by religious and other nonprofit organizations, and federal covered securities.

18. **B.** The sale of these registered securities to an individual would not be an exempt transaction.

19. **B.** The term *federal covered security* specifically applies to any security listed on a major stock exchange or the Nasdaq Stock Market.

20. **B.** Under Section 305(l) of the Uniform Securities Act, the Administrator may require that a prospectus be sent or given to each person to whom an offer is made before the sale of the security.

QUICK QUIZ ANSWERS

Quick Quiz 2.A

1. **C.** Commodity futures contracts and fixed payment life insurance contracts are included in our list of 6 items that are not securities. Commodity option contracts are securities.

2. **C.** Management activity on the part of the owner is not part of the Howey, or 4-part, test for an instrument to be a security. The 4 parts are: (1) an investment of money in (2) a common enterprise with (3) an expectation of profit (4) solely from the effort of others.

3. **C.** Nonexempt securities usually are required to be registered, but not always. If the nonexempt security is sold in an exempt transaction, registration may not be required.

4. **B.** A nonissuer transaction is one in which the company that is the issuer of the security does not receive the proceeds from the transaction. A nonissuer transaction is a transaction between two investors and may or may not require the security to be registered. Whenever the proceeds go to the issuer, it is an issuer transaction.

Quick Quiz 2.B

1. **T.** Registration by coordination involves coordinating a state registration with that of a federal registration.

2. **T.** Any company may register by qualification. Companies that are not established or that intend to offer their securities in 1 state register by qualification.

Quick Quiz 2.C

1. **D.** All of the securities are federal covered securities and therefore are not subject to the registration and advertising filing requirements of the USA.

2. **D.** Variable annuities (whose performance depends on the securities in a segregated fund) are nonexempt, which means they are covered by the act and have to be registered. Securities issued by regulated public utilities, charitable organizations, and banks that are members of the Federal Reserve System are exempt under the USA.

Quick Quiz 2.D

1. **Y.** Mr. Thompson's receipt of an unsolicited order from Ms. Gordon is an exempt transaction.

2. **Y.** The sale of an unregistered security in a private, nonpublicly advertised transaction to 10 or fewer offerees over the last 12 months is an exempt transaction (a private placement).

3. **Y.** The sale of unclaimed securities by certain persons, such as a sheriff or marshal, is an exempt transaction.

4. **N.** The sale of stock of a privately owned company to the public in an initial public offering is not an exempt transaction.

5. **C.** The private placement exemption is limited to 10-noninstitutional offerees, so 14 purchasers would certainly be over the limit. While a security issued by a foreign government with which we have diplomatic relations is an exempt security, a solicited sale by an agent to an individual client is not an exempt transaction.

Quick Quiz 2.E

1. **C.** The USA requires that any application for registration include the amount of securities to be sold in that state. The Administrator has the power to request regular filings of reports, but no more frequently than quarterly. Although the issuer is most commonly the registrant, selling stockholders and broker/dealers may also make application.

UNIT

3

Remedies and Administrative Provisions

The USA is model legislation for the states to use in writing their own securities laws. On your exam, you will not be tested on the specifics of your state's securities laws but on the principles of state regulation laid out in the USA.

This Unit addresses the administrative provisions of the act and the remedies available to the Administrator. Under the USA, the state Administrator has jurisdiction over securities transactions that originate in, are directed into, or are accepted in the Administrator's state.

When a securities transaction falls within the Administrator's jurisdiction, the Administrator has power to make rules and orders; conduct investigations and issue subpoenas; issue cease and desist orders; and deny, suspend, or revoke registrations.

Both civil liabilities and criminal penalties exist for violating the act.

The Series 63 exam will include six questions on the material presented in this Unit. ∎

When you have completed this Unit, you should be able to:

- **describe** the relationship between state and national securities laws;

- **recognize** the jurisdiction of the state securities Administrator;

- **list** the powers of the Administrator within his jurisdiction;

- **describe** the rights of recovery for a security's sale or for investment advice purchased in violation of the USA; and

- **contrast** civil and criminal penalties for violation of the act.

3. 1 AUTHORITY OF THE ADMINISTRATOR

The primary role of the Administrator is to administer the securities laws of the state as well as make rules and issue orders in the public interest to ensure a well functioning investment climate in the state.

As we have already covered, the Administrator deals with registration of securities professionals and securities. In this Unit, we will concentrate on the scope of his authority, frequently referred to as his **jurisdiction** on the exam, and the penalties for those who run afoul of the law.

3. 1. 1   OFFER OR OFFER TO SELL AND SALE OR SELL

We have defined these terms in Unit 1 but need to go into further detail here because the Administrator's authority revolves around offers and sales of securities.

3. 1. 1. 1   Offer or Offer to Sell

The USA defines **offer** or **offer to sell** as every attempt or offer to dispose of, or solicitation of an offer to buy, a security or interest in a security for value. These terms include any:

- security given or delivered with, or as a bonus on account of, any purchase of securities or other items constituting part of the purchase;
- gift of assessable stock (assessable stock is stock issued below par for which the issuer or creditors have the right to assess shareholders for the balance of unpaid par); or
- warrant or right to purchase or subscribe to another security (an offer of the other security is considered to be included in the warrant or right).

3. 1. 1. 2   Sale or Sell

The USA defines **sale** or **sell** as every contract of sale, contract to sell, and disposition of a security or interest in a security for value. This means that any transfer of a security in which money or some other valuable consideration is involved is covered by this definition and subject to the act.

 TAKE NOTE

You must be able to distinguish between a sale and an offer to sell. The offer is the attempt; a transaction has not taken place. In a sale, there has been an actual transaction involving money or another form of consideration for value. One must be properly registered to both make a sale and make the offer.

EXAMPLE

If a car dealer, as an essential part of a sale, offers $1,000 in corporate bonds as an incentive, this would be considered a bonus under the act; therefore, this sale falls under the jurisdiction of the state securities Administrator. As a result, to do this, the car dealer, believe it or not, would have to register with the state as a broker/dealer.

3. 1. 1. 3   Gifts of Assessable Stock

When **assessable** stock is given as a gift, the Administrator has jurisdiction over the transaction because there is a potential future obligation in that either the issuer or, more likely, creditors can demand payment for the balance of the par value. For example, if an individual owned assessable stock and felt that the issuer was on the verge of bankruptcy, that person could give the stock as a present. If the bankruptcy occurred, the new owner would then be subject to the assessment. That, at least in the eyes of the law, means that this is an offer and sale rather than a gift.

TEST TOPIC ALERT   Assessable stock no longer exists, but the exam may ask about it. Look for this direct quote from the Uniform Securities Act: "A purported gift of assessable stock is considered to involve an offer and sale."

3. 1. 1. 4   Exclusions From the Terms Offer, Offer to Sell, Sale, or Sell

The terms *offer* and *offer to sell*, and *sell* or *sale* do not include any:

- bona fide pledge or loan (pledging stock as collateral for a loan, such as in a margin account, is not a sale, nor is lending stock for someone to sell short. In both cases, you expect to get your stock back—you haven't sold it);
- gift of non-assessable stock (this is the way all stocks are today);
- stock dividend or stock split, if nothing of value is given by the stockholders for the additional shares;
- class vote by stockholders, pursuant to the certificate of incorporation or the applicable corporation statute, or a merger, consolidation, reclassification of securities, or sale of corporate assets in consideration of the issuance of securities of another corporation; or
- act incidental to a judicially approved reorganization with which a security is issued in exchange for one or more outstanding securities, claims, or property interest, or partly in such exchange and partly for cash.

TEST TOPIC ALERT   Because you have just learned that the gift of nonassessable stock is not considered a sale, you have to be careful not to be tricked by a question on the exam in which shares of nonassessable stock are given free as a bonus with the purchase of something else (e.g., a security, a car, a house). This would not be a gift and would, in fact, be an offer or a sale.

3. 1. 2   LEGAL JURISDICTION OF THE ADMINISTRATOR

Under law, for any agent of a state (e.g., the Administrator) to have authority over an activity such as a sale or offer of securities, he must have legal jurisdiction to act. **Jurisdiction** under the USA specifically means the legal authority to regulate securities activities that take place in the state.

The USA describes activities considered to have taken place in the state as any offer to buy or sell a security, as well as any acceptance of the offer, if the offer:

- originated in the Administrator's state;
- is directed to the Administrator's state; or
- is accepted in the Administrator's state.

TAKE NOTE

Because securities transactions often involve several states, more than one Administrator may have jurisdiction over a security or a transaction.

CASE STUDY

Offer Originated in Administrator's State

Situation: Mr. Thompson (a registered agent in Illinois), on the recommendation of his best client (Mr. Bixby), phones Ms. Gordon, a friend of Mr. Bixby's who is a resident of Indiana. After having Ms. Gordon open an account with his broker/dealer, Mr. Thompson sells a security to Ms. Gordon, who then mails payment to Mr. Thompson's office in Illinois.

Analysis: The Administrators of both Illinois and Indiana have jurisdiction—the Administrator of Illinois has jurisdiction because the call (offer) originated in Illinois, and the Administrator of Indiana has jurisdiction because the offer was accepted by Ms. Gordon in Indiana.

CASE STUDY

Offer Directed to Administrator's State

Situation: The day after he completes his first transaction with Ms. Gordon, Mr. Thompson mails sales offering materials to her home address in Indiana. Ms. Gordon is not in a position to buy more securities, so she discards the material without reading it.

Analysis: By sending sales materials to Ms. Gordon's home address in Indiana, Mr. Thompson directed the offer to Indiana. Even though Ms. Gordon discarded the information, the Administrator in Indiana has jurisdiction because the sales offer was directed to Indiana. The Administrator of Illinois also has jurisdiction because the offer originated in Illinois. Therefore, if the offering materials were not proper, both Administrators could take action against Mr. Thompson.

3. 1. 2. 1   Publishing and Broadcast Exceptions to Jurisdiction

There are special rules regarding the Administrator's jurisdiction over offers made through a TV or radio broadcast or a bona fide newspaper.

The Administrator would not have jurisdiction if the offer were made under any of the following circumstances:

- Television or radio broadcast that originated outside of the state

- Bona fide newspaper or periodical published outside of the state
- Newspaper or periodical published inside the state that has more than two-thirds (66%) of its circulation outside the state in the last year

TAKE NOTE

A bona fide newspaper is a newspaper of general interest and circulation, such as *The New York Times*. Private investment advisory newsletters, usually distributed by subscription, are not bona fide newspapers and therefore are not included in the publishing exception.

CASE STUDY

Publishing and Broadcast Exemptions

Situation: First Securities & Co., broker/dealers with offices in New York state and Illinois, offers to sell shares in a new retail shoe store chain located in New York. First Securities advertises the offering to residents of New York in the local newspaper, the *New York Gazette*. First Securities also advertises through the *Gazette's* wholly owned radio station. The *Gazette* and its radio station are located in western New York near the Pennsylvania border. About 55% of the *Gazette's* readers and listeners live in Pennsylvania.

Analysis: Although more than half the readers and listeners of the *Gazette* live in Pennsylvania, under the terms of the publishing and broadcasting exemption of the USA, the offer is not made in Pennsylvania because the paper is not published in Pennsylvania. Therefore, the Administrator of New York state has sole jurisdiction over the offering. No dual or multiple jurisdiction applies in this case, unless the offer is actually accepted in Pennsylvania. The fact that First Securities is registered in Illinois in addition to New York is not relevant to this offering because no securities were sold there, nor were any offers or advertising directed to the state.

QUICK QUIZ 3.A

1. A state's securities Administrator has jurisdiction over a securities offering if it
    A. was directed to residents of that state
    B. was originated in that state
    C. was accepted in that state
    D. any of the above

2. An Administrator has jurisdiction over an offer to sell securities if it is made in a newspaper published within the state with no more than
    A. ⅓ of its circulation outside the state
    B. ½ of its circulation outside the state
    C. ⅔ of its circulation outside the state
    D. 90% of its circulation outside the state

Quick Quiz answers can be found at the end of the Unit.

3. 2 ACTIONS TO BE TAKEN BY THE ADMINISTRATOR

The USA not only establishes the jurisdiction of the Administrator but also outlines the powers or the actions that the Administrator can take within its jurisdiction.

The four broad powers the Administrator has to enforce and administer the act in his state are to:

- make, amend, or rescind rules and orders and require the use of specific forms;
- conduct investigations and issue subpoenas;
- issue cease and desist orders and seek injunctions; and
- deny, suspend, cancel, or revoke registrations and licenses.

Although the Administrator has powers to enforce the act for the benefit of the public, the Administrator, as well as his employees, have an obligation not to use the office for personal gain. Administrators are, as a result, prohibited from using, for their own benefit, any information derived from their official duties that has not been made public.

3. 2. 1 RULES, ORDERS, AND FORMS

To enforce the USA, the Administrator has the authority to make, amend, or rescind rules forms, and orders necessary to administer the act. The Administrator may also issue interpretive letters. The USA requires that all rules and forms be published. A rule or order of the Administrator has the same authority as a provision of the act itself, but these rules and orders are not part of the USA itself. The difference between a rule and an order is that a rule applies to everyone, whereas an order applies to a specific instance.

EXAMPLE
The Administrator may decide to issue a rule requiring all agents to pay an annual registration fee of $250. This *rule* applies to everyone. Or, the Administrator may find that a specific agent has violated a provision of the law and orders a 30-day suspension. This *order* applies only to that particular agent.

A person may challenge an order of the Administrator in court within 60 days of order issuance.

Although the Administrator has the power to make and amend rules for compliance with his state's blue-sky law, he does not have the power to alter the law itself.

The composition or content of state securities law is the responsibility of the state legislature, not of administrative agencies. Rules for administration and compliance with the law are the responsibility of the securities Administrator.

CASE STUDY
Rules and Orders of the Administrator

Situation: The Iowa state securities Administrator requires, by rule, that all companies registering their securities in Iowa must supply financial statements in a specific form and with content prescribed by the Administrator. However, the Administrator does not publish the rule because the rule is too long and complex.

Analysis: The USA allows state Administrators to issue rules and orders in carrying out their regulatory functions, and the Iowa Administrator acted properly in designing the form and content for financial reports. However, the USA requires that Administrators publish all rules and orders. The Administrator, despite the latitude he has in administering the USA, cannot suspend any provision of the USA itself. The Iowa Administrator acted within his authority in designing the forms but acted without authority (i.e., he violated the USA) in suspending the requirement that all rules and orders be published.

3. 2. 2   CONDUCT INVESTIGATIONS AND ISSUE SUBPOENAS

The Administrator has broad discretionary authority to conduct investigations and issue subpoenas. These investigations may be made in public or in private and may occur within or outside of the Administrator's state. Normally, these investigations are open to the public, but when, in the opinion of the Administrator and with the consent of all parties, it is felt that a private investigation is more appropriate, that investigation will be conducted without public scrutiny.

In conducting an investigation, the Administrator, or any officer designated by him, has the power to:

■ require statements in writing, under oath, regarding all matters relating to the issue under investigation;

■ publish and make public the facts and circumstances concerning the issue to be investigated;

■ subpoena witnesses and compel their attendance and testimony; and

■ take evidence and require the production of books, papers, correspondence, and any other documents deemed relevant.

3. 2. 2. 1   Contumacy

So, what happens if a person who is the subject of an investigation refuses to furnish the required evidence or just ignores the subpoena? After all, the Administrator is not a police officer—he doesn't "wear a badge" and cannot arrest anyone. There is a legal term that describes this type of disobedience. That term is **contumacy** and here is what the USA says about that:

In case of contumacy by, or refusal to obey a subpoena issued to, any person, the Administrator may apply to the appropriate court in his state and ask for help. Upon application by the Administrator, the court can issue an order to the person requiring him to appear before the Administrator, or the officer designated by him, to produce documentary evidence if so ordered or to give evidence touching the matter under investigation or in question. Failure to obey the order of the court may be punished by the court as a contempt of court.

Contempt of court can, of course, lead to jail time.

TAKE NOTE

In addition to having the power to conduct investigations, the Administrator may enforce subpoenas issued by Administrators in other states on the same basis as if the alleged offense took place in the Administrator's state. However, the Administrator may issue and apply to enforce subpoenas in his state at the request of a securities agency or administrator of another state only if the activities constituting an alleged violation for which the information is sought would be a violation of the USA if the activities had occurred in his state.

3. 2. 3   ISSUE CEASE AND DESIST ORDERS

If an Administrator determines that a person is about to engage in an activity that constitutes a violation of the USA or her rules, the Administrator may issue a cease and desist order without a hearing. The Administrator is granted this power to prevent potential violations before they occur. It is sometimes said that the Administrator can act when she "smells the smoke, even without seeing the fire." Sometimes a tipster or whistleblower will divulge information to the Administrator that might be relevant to a serious infraction. To prevent any further damage to investors, a cease and desist order can be entered.

Although the Administrator has the power to issue cease and desist orders, she does not have the legal power to compel compliance with the order. To compel compliance in the face of a person's resistance, the Administrator must apply to a court of competent jurisdiction for an injunction. Only the courts can compel compliance by issuing injunctions and imposing penalties for violation of them. You will need to know that **enjoined** is the legal term that is used to refer to a person who is the subject of an injunction. If a temporary or permanent injunction is issued, upon request of the Administrator, a receiver or conservator may be appointed over the defendant's assets.

TAKE NOTE

Cease and desist orders are not the same as stop orders. Cease and desist orders are directed to persons, requiring them to cease activities. Stop orders are directed to applications regarding registration of a security. Furthermore, stop orders require a hearing while cease and desist orders do not.

CASE STUDY   **Cease and Desist Orders**

Situation: Mr. Thompson is registered to conduct business in the state of Illinois and makes plans to sell a security within the next few days. The Administrator considers this security ineligible for sale in the state. The Administrator orders Mr. Thompson to stop his sales procedures immediately.

Analysis: The Administrator of Illinois issued a cease and desist order to Mr. Thompson because there was not sufficient time to conduct a public hearing before the sale to determine whether the security was eligible for sale in the state.

Frequently, before a final determination of proceedings under the act, the Administrator will act summarily to suspend a registration. However, no formal order may be issued without the Administrator:

- giving appropriate prior notice to the affected persons;
- granting an opportunity for a hearing; and
- providing findings of fact and conclusions of law.

3. 2. 4   DENY, SUSPEND, CANCEL, OR REVOKE REGISTRATIONS

The Administrator also has the power to deny, suspend, cancel, or revoke the registration of broker/dealers, investment advisers, and their representatives, as well as the registration of securities issues.

3. 2. 4. 1   Broker/Dealers, Advisers, and their Representatives

To justify a denial, revocation, or suspension of the license of a **securities professional**, the Administrator must find that the order is in the public interest and also find that the applicant or registrant, or in the case of a broker/dealer or investment adviser, any partner, officer, or director, or any person occupying a similar status or performing similar functions:

- has filed an incomplete, false, or misleading registration application;
- has willfully violated the USA;
- has been convicted of a securities-related misdemeanor within the last 10 years;
- has been convicted of any felony within the last 10 years;
- has been enjoined by law from engaging in the securities business;
- is subject to any other Administrator's denial, revocation, or suspension;
- is engaged in dishonest or unethical securities practices;
- is insolvent;
- has, in the case of a broker/dealer or investment adviser, been found guilty on the charge of failure to supervise;
- has failed to pay application filing fees; and
- is not qualified because of lack of training, experience, or knowledge of the securities business.

TEST TOPIC ALERT   Because of a lack of uniformity in state criminal laws, it can happen that one is convicted of a misdemeanor in one state and then moves to a state where that same crime is a felony. If the person were to then apply for registration, the Administrator must consider the crime under the statutes of the state where it occurred, not his own. In other words, the Administrator may only consider what is on the person's record.

The Administrator must notify the registrant of any reason to deny, suspend, revoke, or cancel a registration and, if asked in writing, must provide a hearing within 15 days. In addition, if the registrant is an agent or an IAR, the employing broker/dealer or IA, respectively, will receive notice of the final order from the Administrator. The Administrator may not stop a registration on the basis of facts that were known to the Administrator at the time the registration became effective (unless the proceedings are initiated within 30 days).

3. 2. 4. 2   Securities Issues

As is the case with a securities professional, a securities Administrator may deny, suspend, cancel, or revoke a security's registration if the order is in the public's interest and the securities registrant:

- files a misleading or incomplete registration statement;

- is engaged in an offering that is fraudulent or made on unfair, unjust, or inequitable terms;

- charges offering fees that are excessive or unreasonable;

- has a control person convicted of a securities-related crime;

- is subject to a court injunction;

- is engaged in a method of business that is illegal; or

- is subject to an administrative stop order of any other state.

In addition, the Administrator may deny a registration if the applicant fails to pay the filing fee. When the fee is paid, the denial order will be removed, provided the applicant is in compliance with all registration procedures.

1. With regard to the powers of the Administrator, which of the following statements are NOT true?

   I. The Administrator must seek an injunction to issue a cease and desist order.
   II. The USA requires an Administrator to conduct a full hearing, public or private, before issuing a cease and desist order.
   III. The USA grants the Administrator the power to issue injunctions to force compliance with the provisions of the act.
   A. I and II
   B. I and III
   C. II and III
   D. I, II and III

2. Although the Administrator has great power, the USA does place some limitations on the office. Which of the following statements regarding those powers are TRUE?

   I. In conducting an investigation, an Administrator can compel the testimony of witnesses.
   II. Investigations of serious violations must be open to the public.
   III. An Administrator in Illinois may enforce subpoenas from South Carolina only if the violation originally occurred in Illinois.
   IV. An Administrator may deny the registration of a securities professional who has been convicted of a felony within the past 10 years but must provide, if requested in writing, a hearing within 15 days.
   A. I, II and IV
   B. I, III and IV
   C. I and IV
   D. II and III

3. 2. 5   NONPUNITIVE TERMINATIONS OF REGISTRATION

A registration can be terminated even if there has not been a violation of the USA. A request for withdrawal and lack of qualification are both reasons for cancellation.

3. 2. 5. 1   Withdrawal

A person may request on his own initiative a withdrawal of a registration. The withdrawal is effective 30 days after the Administrator receives it, provided no revocation or suspension proceedings are in process against the person making the request. In that event, the Administrator may institute a revocation or suspension proceeding within one year after a withdrawal becomes effective.

TEST TOPIC ALERT   Once your registration has been withdrawn, the Administrator still retains jurisdiction over you for a period of one year.

3. 2. 5. 2   Lack of Qualification

An Administrator may not base a denial of a person's registration solely on his lack of experience. However, the Administrator may consider that registration as a broker/dealer does not necessarily qualify one for a license as an investment adviser and may restrict that applicant's registration as a broker/dealer conditional upon its not functioning as an investment adviser.

To better understand these two points, let's look at the wording in the Act itself:

1. The Administrator may not enter an order denying registration solely on the basis of lack of experience *if* the applicant or registrant is qualified by training or knowledge or both.

   Obviously, a new applicant for registration as an agent is not going to have any experience selling securities. So, the Act says that this lack of experience by itself is not enough to deny the registration as long as the Administrator feels assured that the individual will receive adequate training and/or has the requisite knowledge. One could suppose that passing this exam demonstrates the necessary "knowledge."

2. The Administrator may consider that an investment adviser is not necessarily qualified solely on the basis of experience as a broker/dealer or agent. When he finds that an applicant for initial or renewal registration as a broker/dealer is not qualified as an investment adviser, he may, by order, condition the applicant's registration as a broker/dealer upon his not transacting business in this state as an investment adviser.

   In this case, the Act is dealing with a person who has experience, albeit not necessarily in the giving of advice. Just because a person has been a broker/dealer, or an agent for a broker/dealer, does not mean that the person is qualified to be an investment adviser. So, the registration will be limited to acting only in their stated capacity as long as one does not cross over the line and give investment advice.

3. 2. 5. 3   Cancellation

If an Administrator finds that an applicant or a registrant no longer exists or has ceased to transact business, the Administrator may cancel the registration.

TEST TOPIC ALERT   You may encounter this type of question regarding cancellation: "What would the Administrator do if mailings to a registrant were returned with no forwarding address?" The answer is, "Cancel the registration."

The Administrator may also cancel a registration if a person is declared mentally incompetent.

TAKE NOTE   Be familiar with the distinction between cancellation and denial, suspension, or revocation. Cancellation does not result from violations or a failure to follow the provisions of the act. Cancellation occurs as the result of death, dissolution, or mental incompetency and, unlike the others, is not a form of punishment.

1. Which of the following statements relating to termination of registration is TRUE?
   A. A registration, once in effect, may never be voluntarily withdrawn.
   B. An Administrator may not cancel a registration of a securities professional who is declared mentally incompetent.
   C. An Administrator may revoke the registration of a securities professional who is declared mentally incompetent.
   D. An Administrator may cancel the registration of a registrant no longer in business.

3. 3   PENALTIES AND LIABILITIES

The USA provides both civil liabilities and criminal penalties for persons who violate the USA. In addition, the act provides for recovery by a client of financial loss that results from the fraudulent sale of a security or investment advice.

3. 3. 1   CIVIL LIABILITIES

Persons who sell securities or offer investment advice in violation of the USA are subject to civil liabilities (as well as possible criminal penalties).

The purchaser of securities sold in violation of the act may sue the seller to recover financial loss.

The purchaser can sue for recovery if the:

- securities were sold in violation of the registration provisions of the USA;
- securities professional omitted or made an untrue statement of material fact;
- securities were sold by an agent who should have been but was not registered under the act; or
- securities were sold in violation of a rule or order of the securities Administrator.

Although most civil suits are brought by the purchaser, the administrator may bring a civil enforcement action in a court, particularly to prevent publication, circulation, or use of any materials required by the administrator to be filed under the Act that have not been filed.

TEST TOPIC ALERT

Unlike some federal laws, there is no provision for receiving "treble" damages. That is, in addition to receiving back your investment, you receive payment equal to three times what you lost. That is primarily found in the federal laws regarding insider trading, but that is not relevant to this exam.

3. 3. 1. 1   Statute of Limitations

The time limit, or **statute of limitations**, for violations of the civil provisions of the USA is three years from the date of sale (or rendering of investment advice) or two years after discovering the violation, whichever occurred first.

TEST TOPIC ALERT   Every cause of action under this statute survives the death of any person who might have been a plaintiff or defendant.

3. 3. 1. 2   Rights of Recovery from Improper Sale of Securities

The person buying the security from any person who makes a sale in violation may request rescission and, if the seller refuses, may sue (as long as it is within the statute of limitations) to recover the consideration paid for the security, together with interest at (x) percent per year from the date of payment for the purchase, court costs, and reasonable attorneys' fees, less the amount of any income received on the security. So, the buyer will be made "whole" plus interest (less any income already received) plus all legal costs.

3. 3. 1. 3   Right of Rescission for Securities Sales

If the seller of securities discovers that he has made a sale in violation of the USA, the seller may offer to repurchase the securities from the buyer. In this case, the seller is offering the buyer the **right of rescission**. To satisfy the buyer's right of rescission, the amount paid back to the buyer must include the original purchase price and interest at a rate determined by the Administrator.

By offering to buy back the securities that were sold in violation of the act, the seller can avoid a lawsuit (and the payment of court costs and legal fees) through a **letter of rescission**. The buyer has 30 days after receiving the letter of rescission to respond. If the buyer does not accept or reject the rescission offer within 30 days, the buyer forfeits the right to pursue a lawsuit at a later date.

If the buyer accepts the rescission offer, he may recover:

■ the original purchase price of the securities;

■ plus interest at a rate determined by the Administrator (generally referred to as the state's *legal rate*);

■ minus income received during the period in which the securities were held.

TAKE NOTE   If the client rejects the offer within the 30-day period, he may sue. In the real world, this almost never happens because there is very little chance that he would receive any greater amount than what is being offered under rescission.

3. 3. 1. 4   Rights of Recovery from Improper Investment Advice

A person who buys a security as the result of investment advice received in violation of the USA also has the right to sue. In the case of securities purchased as a result of improper investment advice, the buyer may recover:

■ the cost of the advice;

■ plus losses resulting from the advice;

■ plus all interest costs from the date of fee payment at a rate determined by the Administrator;

- plus any reasonable attorney's fees;
- less the amount of any income received from such advice.

3. 3. 1. 5 Right of Rescission for Investment Advice

Similar to the right of rescission described above for securities sales, an investment adviser who realizes that he has given advice that will subject him to civil action may avoid legal expenses by offering the client the same package as he would receive if he had sued. That is, refunding the cost of the advice, losses from the advice, and interest at the state's predetermined rate, less any income received on recommended securities.

3. 3. 1. 6 Scope of Liability

Under the USA, the actual seller of the securities or the advice is not the only person liable for the violation of the act. Every person who directly or indirectly controls the person who sold the securities or the advice, or is a material aid to the transaction, is also liable to the same extent as the person who conducted the transaction.

The effect of this is that if an agent makes a sale in violation (or IAR gives improper advice), but it can be shown that officers or partners of the broker/dealer or IA were irresponsible, action can be taken against them as well, and they can be found civilly liable.

TAKE NOTE   When securities are sold improperly, the buyer can recover the original purchase price in addition to reasonable income plus, if suit is necessary, legal costs. When improper investment advice is offered, the purchaser of the advice is entitled to recover the cost of the advice, losses incurred, and legal costs, but is not entitled to recover the original purchase price from the adviser.

3. 3. 1. 7 Surety Bond

In Unit 1, we discussed the need for securities professionals to post a surety bond under certain conditions. The USA states, "every bond shall provide for suit thereon by any person who has a cause of action under this Act and, if the Administrator by rule or order requires, by any person who has a cause of action not arising under this act. Every bond shall provide that no suit may be maintained to enforce any liability on the bond unless brought within the time limitations of the Act." In other words, in order for a surety bond to meet the requirements of the Uniform Securities Act, it must provide that any customer who can prove a violation, (and does so within the statute of limitations), is entitled to collect against the bond.

TAKE NOTE   Because this is an exam based on the law, it is sometimes necessary for us to delve into the legalities more than we would like. The USA states: "Any person who offers or sells a security in violation of the Act is liable to the person buying the security from him." What this does is impose civil liability when the offer violates one of the specified provisions even though the sale does not. The making of a nonexempted offer before the effective date can create no civil rights on behalf of the offeree (the potential buyer) unless the offer results in a sale. When it does, however, this language means that the buyer may recover even though no contract was made until after the effective date.

3. 3. 2   CRIMINAL PENALTIES

Persons found guilty of a fraudulent securities transaction are subject to criminal penalties (as well as possible civil liabilities). Upon conviction, a person may be fined, imprisoned, or both. The maximum penalty is a fine of $5,000, a jail sentence of three years, or both. It is important to note that no person may be imprisoned for the violation of any rule or order if he proves that he had no knowledge of the rule or order. In other words, you have to know that you are willingly in violation in order to get jail time. It is also important to note that while the Administrator does not have the power to arrest anyone, he may apply to the appropriate authorities in his state for the issuance of an arrest warrant. The appropriate state prosecutor, usually the State Attorney General, may decide whether to bring a criminal action under the USA, another statute, or, when applicable, common law. In certain states, the Administrator has full or limited criminal enforcement powers. To be convicted of fraud, the violation must be willful and the registrant must know that the activity is fraudulent.

TAKE NOTE   **Fraud** is the deliberate or willful concealment, misrepresentation, or omission of material information or the truth to deceive or manipulate another person for unlawful or unfair gain. Under the USA, fraud is not limited to common-law deceit.

3. 3. 2. 1   Statute of Limitations

The statute of limitations for criminal offenses under the USA is five years from the date of the offense.

TAKE NOTE   Remember the sequence 5-5-3 for the application of criminal penalties: 5-year statute of limitations, $5,000 maximum fine, and imprisonment of no more than 3 years.

Under the civil provisions, the statute of limitations is 2 years from the discovery of the offense or 3 years after the act occurred, whichever occurs first.

CASE STUDY   **Fraudulent Sale of Securities**

Situation: Mr. Thompson, the registered sales agent, knowingly omitted the fact that the shares of a company he sold to his client, Mr. Bixby, were downgraded to speculative grade and that their bonds were placed on a credit watch by one of the major credit rating agencies. A month after the sale, the shares became worthless.

Analysis: Mr. Thompson sold these securities to Mr. Bixby in violation of the USA because he deliberately or knowingly failed to mention material information—information that was important for Mr. Bixby to know to make an informed investment decision. Mr. Bixby has the right to recover the financial losses that resulted from the sale. Not only that, but the Administrator could apply to the appropriate court to take criminal action.

3. 3. 3   JUDICIAL REVIEW OF ORDERS (APPEAL)

Any person affected by an order of the Administrator may obtain a review of the order in an appropriate court by filing a written petition within 60 days. **In general,** filing an appeal does not automatically act as a stay of the penalty. The order will go into effect as issued unless the court rules otherwise.

QUICK QUIZ 3.D

1. Which of the following statements relating to penalties under the USA is TRUE?

    A. Unknowing violation of the USA by an agent is cause for imprisonment under the criminal liability provisions of the act.
    B. If a violation has occurred in the sale of a security, the purchaser of the security may recover the original purchase price, legal costs, and interest, less any earnings already received.
    C. A seller who notices that a sale was made in violation of the act may offer a right of rescission to the purchaser; the purchaser must accept this right within the earlier of two years after notice of the violation or three years after the sale.
    D. Any person aggrieved by an order of the Administrator may request an appeal of the order within 15 days which, in effect, functions as a stay of the order during the appeal period.

2. When making an offer of a new issue that is in registration to a prospective client, an agent claims that his registration with the Administrator is proof of his qualifications. Under the USA

    A. claiming his registration is approved by the Administrator while making an offer of a security undergoing registration subjects this agent to a civil liability claim
    B. claiming his registration is approved by the Administrator while making an offer of a security does not subject this agent to a civil liability claim until the registration becomes effective
    C. claiming his registration is approved by the Administrator subjects this agent only to civil liability if a sale results
    D. regardless of whether a sale takes place, an agent making a misleading statement of this type subjects himself to possible civil liability

3. 4 OTHER PROVISIONS

In addition to the items previously mentioned, there are several miscellaneous provisions under the Administrator's authority.

3. 4. 1 FILING OF SALES AND ADVERTISING LITERATURE

The Administrator may by rule or order, (remember, there is a difference between those two terms), require the filing of any prospectus, pamphlet, circular, form letter, advertisement, or other sales literature or advertising communication addressed or intended for distribution to prospective investors, including clients or prospective clients of an investment adviser unless the security is exempt, the transaction is exempt, or is a federal covered security.

3. 4. 2 ADMINISTRATIVE FILES AND OPINIONS

A document is considered to be filed when it is received by the Administrator.

3. 4. 2. 1 Maintenance of Records

The Administrator maintains a record of all applications for registration of securities and registration statements and all applications for broker/dealer, agent, investment adviser, or investment adviser representative registration which are or have ever been effective in his state; all written notices of claim of exemption from registration requirements; all orders entered under this act; and all interpretative opinions or no-action determinations issued. All records may be maintained in computer or microfilm format or any other form of data storage. The record is available for public inspection. The information contained in or filed with any registration statement, application, or report may be made available to the public under such rules as the Administrator prescribes.

3. 4. 2. 2 Availability of Copies

Upon request and at such reasonable charges as he prescribes, the Administrator shall furnish to any person photostatic or other copies (certified under his seal of office if requested) of any entry in the register or any document which is a matter of public record. In any proceeding or prosecution under this act, any copy so certified is prima facie evidence of the contents of the entry or document certified.

3. 4. 2. 3 Interpretive Opinions

The Administrator, in his discretion, may honor requests from interested persons for interpretative opinions or may issue determinations that the Administrator will not institute enforcement proceedings against certain specified persons for engaging in certain specified activities where the determination is consistent with the purposes fairly intended by the policy and provisions of this act. The Administrator may charge a fee for interpretative opinions and no-action determinations. This is similar to the same procedure used for "letter rulings" from the IRS.

UNIT TEST

1. If convicted of a willful violation of the Uniform Securities Act, an agent is subject to

   A. imprisonment for 5 years
   B. a fine of $5,000 and/or imprisonment for 3 years
   C. a fine of $10,000
   D. disbarment

2. To protect the public, the Administrator may

   I. deny a registration if the registrant does not have sufficient experience to function as an agent
   II. limit a registrant's functions to those of a broker/dealer if, in the initial application for registration as an investment adviser, the registrant is not qualified to act as an adviser
   III. take into consideration in approving a registration that the registrant will work under the supervision of a registered investment adviser or broker/dealer
   IV. deny a registration, although denial is not in the public's interest, if it is prudent in view of a change in the state's political composition

   A. I and II
   B. II and III
   C. III and IV
   D. I, II, III and IV

3. Aaron is a client of XYZ Financial Services. Over the past several years, Aaron has been suspicious of possible churning of his account but has taken no action because account performance has been outstanding. After reviewing his most recent statement, Aaron suspects that excessive transactions have occurred. He consults his attorney, who informs him that under the USA, any lawsuit for recovery of damages under the USA must be started within

   A. 1 year of occurrence
   B. 2 years of occurrence
   C. 3 years of occurrence or 2 years of discovery, whichever occurs first
   D. 2 years of occurrence or 3 years of discovery, whichever occurs last

4. Which of the following accurately describes a cease and desist order as authorized by the USA?

   A. An order that a federal agency issued to a brokerage firm to stop an advertising campaign
   B. An Administrator's order to refrain from a practice of business he believes to be unfair
   C. A court-issued order requiring a business to stop an unfair practice
   D. An order from one brokerage firm to another to refrain from unfair business practices

5. A customer living in one state receives a phone call from an agent in another state. A transaction between the two occurs in yet another state. According to the Uniform Securities Act, under whose jurisdiction does the transaction fall?

   A. Administrator of the state in which the customer lives
   B. Administrator of the state from which the agent made the call
   C. Administrator of the state in which the transaction took place
   D. Administrators of all 3 states involved

6. By rule, the Administrator may

   A. forbid an adviser from taking custody of client funds
   B. allow an agent to waive provisions of the USA
   C. suspend federal law if he believes it to be in the public interest
   D. suspend the registration of a federal covered adviser because the contract did not meet the requirements for a state-sanctioned investment advisory contract

7. If it is in the public interest, the Uniform Securities Act provides that the state Administrator may deny the registration of a broker/dealer for all of the following reasons EXCEPT

    A. the applicant is not qualified because of lack of experience
    B. a willful violation of the Uniform Securities Act has taken place
    C. the applicant is financially insolvent
    D. the applicant is enjoined temporarily from engaging in the securities business

8. If an agent chooses to appeal an Administrator's order, when must the agent file for review of the order with the appropriate court?

    A. Immediately
    B. Within 30 days after the entry of the order
    C. Within 60 days after the entry of the order
    D. Within 180 days after the entry of the order

9. An Administrator may summarily suspend a registration pending final determination of proceedings under the USA. However, the Administrator may not enter a final order without

    I. appropriate prior notice to the applicant as well as the employer or prospective employer of the applicant
    II. opportunity for a hearing
    III. findings of fact and conclusions of law
    IV. prior written acknowledgment of the applicant
    A. I only
    B. I and II
    C. I, II and III
    D. I, II, III and IV

10. The Administrator has authority to

    I. issue a cease and desist order without a hearing
    II. issue a cease and desist order only after a hearing
    III. suspend a securities registration upon discovering an officer of the registrant has been convicted of a nonsecurities-related crime that is listed on the officer's police record as a misdemeanor
    IV. sentence violators of the USA to 3 years in prison
    A. I only
    B. I and IV
    C. II and III
    D. II and IV

11. Which of the following statements regarding NASAA Guidelines is NOT true?

    A. The Administrator's rules apply to general situations.
    B. The Administrator's orders apply to specific situations.
    C. The Administrator may work in concert with the SEC in developing rules and regulations.
    D. At least once every 5 years, the Administrator's rules are subject to a relevancy review.

12. An agent lives in Montana and is registered in Montana and Idaho. His broker/dealer is registered in every state west of the Mississippi River. The agent's client, who lives in Montana, decides to enroll in a 1-year resident MBA program in Philadelphia. During the 1-year period when the client is in Philadelphia, the agent may

    A. conduct business with the client as usual
    B. only accept unsolicited orders
    C. not conduct business with the client
    D. not deal with the client until the broker/dealer registers in Pennsylvania

13. An Administrator may deny an investment adviser representative for all of the following reasons EXCEPT

    A. lack of experience
    B. failure to post a surety bond
    C. failure to pass a written exam
    D. not meeting minimum financial standards

14. The Administrator may cancel the registration of an adviser if

    A. mail is returned with a notice that the forwarding notice has expired
    B. the adviser is not in the business any longer
    C. a court has declared the adviser to be mentally incompetent
    D. any of the above

15. An agent of a broker/dealer has been found civilly liable for making untrue statements in connection with a public offering. The officers of the firm purchased a compliance program from a third party software developer that was designed to be able to protect against the untrue statements reaching clients. Unfortunately, the program was never used because they could not figure out how it worked. What is the nature of the civil liability of the officers?

    A. They are liable because they did not act responsibly.
    B. They are only liable if they willingly ignored the untrue statements.
    C. The liability is that of the agent's supervisor, not the officers.
    D. Officers are never liable for actions of their agents.

ANSWERS AND RATIONALES

1. **B.** Under the USA, the maximum penalty is a fine of $5,000 and/or 3 years in jail.

2. **B.** The Administrator may determine that an applicant, in his initial application for registration as an investment adviser, is not qualified to act as an adviser and thus may limit the registration to that of a broker/dealer; the Administrator can also take into consideration whether the registrant will work under the supervision of a registered investment adviser or broker/dealer when approving an application. The Administrator can deny, suspend, or revoke a registration for many reasons, but they must be in the interest of the public. The Administrator may not deny the registration simply because it is prudent. Lack of experience in itself is insufficient reason for denial.

3. **C.** Under the USA, the lawsuit for recovery of damages must commence within the sooner of 3 years of occurrence of the offense or 2 years of its discovery.

4. **B.** A cease and desist order is a directive from an administrative agency to immediately stop a particular action. Administrators may issue cease and desist orders with or without a prior hearing. Brokerage houses cannot issue cease and desist orders to each other.

5. **D.** Under the scope of the Uniform Securities Act, if any part of a transaction occurs in a state, the transaction falls under the jurisdiction of the state Administrator. The transaction is under the control of the Administrator of the state in which the customer lives (because the offer was received there), the Administrator of the state in which the agent is calling (because the offer was made from that state), and the Administrator of the state in which the transaction took place.

6. **A.** The Administrator has considerable discretion to make rules or issue orders. Specifically, the USA allows the Administrator to prohibit custody by rule. However, the USA does not allow the Administrator to waive provisions of the USA, nor can the Administrator suspend federal law.

7. **A.** If the broker/dealer qualifies by virtue of training or knowledge, registration cannot be denied for lack of experience only. Registration may be denied if the applicant willfully violates the Uniform Securities Act, is financially insolvent, or has been enjoined (is the subject of a court issued injunction) from engaging in the securities business.

8. **C.** Under the USA, a registered person has up to 60 days to appeal any order issued against him by the state Administrator.

9. **C.** With the exception of proceedings awaiting final determination, the Administrator must provide appropriate prior notice to the applicant as well as the employer or prospective employer of the applicant and provide the opportunity for a hearing. In addition, the Administrator may issue a final order only after findings of fact and conclusions of law. An applicant is not required to provide written acknowledgment before an order is issued.

10. **A.** The Administrator may issue a cease and desist order without a hearing but does not have the authority to sentence violators of the USA. The Administrator may not suspend a security's registration upon discovering, in subsequent years, that an officer of the firm has been convicted of a nonsecurities-related crime, as long as it is a misdemeanor. Had it been any felony, then suspension of the issue's registration is a possibility.

11. **D.** Relevancy review is not part of the act.

12. **A.** Even though the college program is referred to as a resident program, that does not mean the client has changed his state of residence. Although neither the firm nor the agent is registered, the agent may continue to conduct business with the client because both the agent and his firm are properly registered in the client's state of permanent residence.

13. **A.** Lack of experience, by itself, is not cause for registration denial.

14. **D.** You must know the difference between cancellation of a registration (which requires no hearing) and revocation (which does).

15. **A.** As President Harry Truman famously said, "the buck stops here." Officers carry liability on behalf of the broker/dealer. Had they taken the initiative to learn how to use the compliance program, the agent would have been stopped in his tracks.

QUICK QUIZ ANSWERS

Quick Quiz 3.A

1. **D.** The Administrator has jurisdiction over a security offering if it was directed to, originated in, or was accepted in that state.

2. **C.** A state Administrator has jurisdiction over a securities offering made in a bona fide newspaper published within the state with no more than ⅔ of its circulation outside the state.

Quick Quiz 3.B

1. **D.** The Administrator need not seek an injunction to issue a cease and desist order. The USA does not require that an Administrator conduct a public or private hearing before issuing a cease and desist order. When time does not permit, the Administrator may issue a cease and desist order before a hearing to prevent a pending violation. The USA does not grant the Administrator the power to issue injunctions to force compliance with the act. The act permits the Administrator to issue cease and desist orders, and, if they do not work, the Administrator may seek an injunction from a court of competent jurisdiction. A cease and desist order is an administrative order, whereas an injunction is a judicial order.

2. **C.** An Administrator can compel the testimony of witnesses when conducting an investigation. Investigation of serious violations need not be held in public. An Administrator in Illinois may enforce subpoenas from South Carolina whether the violation occurred in Illinois or not. Conviction for any felony within the past 10 years is one of a number of reasons the Administrator has for denying a license. However, upon notice of the denial, a written request may be made for a hearing. That request must be honored within 15 days.

Quick Quiz 3.C

1. **D.** An Administrator does not revoke the registration of a person who is declared mentally incompetent but cancels such registration; cancellation is a non-punitive administrative action. An administrator may cancel the registration of a registrant that is no longer in existence. A person may request a withdrawal of a registration. Withdrawals become effective after 30 days if there are no revocation or denial proceedings in process.

Quick Quiz 3.D

1. **B.** A client who purchased a security in violation of the USA may recover the original purchase price plus costs involved in filing a lawsuit. In addition, the purchaser is entitled to interest at a rate stated by the Administrator, less any earnings already received on the investment. To be subject to time in prison, a sales agent must knowingly have violated the USA. The right of rescission must be accepted or rejected within 30 days of receipt of the letter of rescission. Although any person aggrieved by an order of the Administrator may request an appeal of the order within 60 days, such appeal does not function as a stay order during the appeal process. The person who is the subject of the order must comply with the order during the period unless a stay is granted by the court.

2. **C.** For an agent to have civil liability, a sale must take place. If the offer is made using a statement like the one in this question and a sale subsequently occurs, a client suffering a loss would be able to sue. Even though one may never claim approval by the Administrator, there is no civil liability unless the client has some kind of a claim. However, even though the client cannot bring a case, the Administrator could bring a disciplinary action against the agent for making this claim. On a law exam, you must be careful to understand who has a claim and when they do.

4

Ethical Practices and Fiduciary Obligations

T he USA was drafted for two primary reasons: (1) to eliminate conflicts in state securities legislation and make state securities laws uniform and (2) to protect the public from fraudulent and unethical securities practices. The protection against fraud, as well as unethical and prohibited practices, is the subject of this Unit. This Unit addresses what constitutes fraudulent practices under securities laws as well as what constitutes unethical and prohibited business practices as defined in the Statements of Policy issued by NASAA, the North American Securities Administrators Association.

Fraudulent, prohibited, and unethical practices are the very heavily tested topics. They make up 40% of the exam. You must know what these practices are and be able to apply the principles that guide ethical behavior to specific situations presented in the exam.

The Series 63 exam will include 24 questions on the material presented in this Unit. ∎

When you have completed this Unit, you should be able to:

- **understand** the antifraud provisions of the USA;

- **recognize** specific fraudulent, unethical, and prohibited practices;

- **make** distinctions between prohibitions that pertain to the sale of securities and prohibitions that pertain to the sale of investment advice;

- **list** the required provisions for investment advisory contracts; and

- **identify** various types of deceptive market manipulation.

4. 1   ANTIFRAUD PROVISIONS OF THE USA

Fraudulent activity may occur when conducting securities sales or when providing investment advice. Each of these categories is discussed separately. In general, **fraud** means the deliberate or willful attempt to deceive someone for profit or gain. As mentioned in previous Units, if it is a security, exempt or not, it is covered under the USA's anti-fraud provisions. However, these provisions only apply to securities. Therefore, if the inappropriate activity occurs during the offer or sale or rendering of advice relating to something that is *not* a security, these anti-fraud provisions do not apply.

4. 1. 1   FRAUDULENT AND PROHIBITED PRACTICES

Although there is a legal difference between a fraudulent practice and one that is unethical or prohibited, it is highly unlikely that you will have to know that for the exam. About the only significant testable concern is that you can go to jail for committing fraud (a criminal offense) while engaging in a practice that is prohibited or unethical is generally limited to a fine, and/or suspension or revocation. Most of the exam will deal with practices that are unethical, but let's point out what the Uniform Securities Act considers fraud.

State securities laws modeled on the USA address fraud by making it unlawful for any person, when engaged in the offer, sale, or purchase of any security, directly or indirectly, to:

- employ any device, scheme, or artifice to defraud;
- make any untrue statement of a material fact or omit to state a material fact necessary to make a statement not misleading; or
- engage in any act, practice, or course of business that operates as a fraud or deceit on a person.

With regard to investment advice, it is unlawful for any person who receives, directly or indirectly, any consideration from another person for advising the other person as to the value of securities or their purchase or sale, whether through the issuance of analyses or reports or otherwise, to:

- employ any device, scheme, or artifice to defraud the other person; or
- engage in any act, practice, or course of business which operates or would operate as a fraud or deceit upon the other person.

There are other more specific examples related to investment advice, but we will cover them as they arise.

TAKE NOTE
As long as it involves a security, there are no exceptions to the antifraud provisions of state securities laws. They pertain to any person or transaction whether the person or transaction is registered, exempt, or federal covered. Prevention of fraud is one of the few areas of securities law over which the states have full authority to act.

The following is a list of the fraudulent acts most likely to be tested on your exam.

4. 1. 1. 1   Misleading or Untrue Statements

Securities laws prohibit any person from making misleading or untrue statements of a material fact in connection with the purchase or sale of a security. Not all facts are material. The law defines **material** as information used by a prospective purchaser to make an informed investment decision. In other words, when selling securities to their clients, agents must not deliberately conceal a material fact to encourage a client to buy or sell a security. Such act would constitute deceit for personal gain.

An agent providing a client with an inaccurate address of a company whose shares the client was interested in purchasing would not be making an untrue statement of a material fact. Investors do not purchase shares on the basis of the company's street address. On the other hand, investors do make investment decisions on the basis of the qualifications of a company's management. Those qualifications would therefore be material fact. To misstate them is fraud. An example would be claiming that the chief operating officer (COO) of a biotech company had a Ph.D. in biochemistry when, in fact, the doctorate was in sociology.

The following are examples of material facts that constitute fraud if misstated by agents knowingly and willfully.

- **Inaccurate market quotations**—Telling a client a stock is up when the reverse is true is obviously an improper action. However, it would not be considered fraud if the inaccuracy resulted from a malfunction of the quote machine or an unintended clerical error. To be considered fraud, the action must be deliberate.

- **Misstatements of an issuer's earnings or projected earnings or dividends**—Telling a client that earnings are up, or that the dividend will be increased when such is not the case, is a fraudulent practice. However, it would not be fraud if you were quoting a news release that was incorrect.

- **Inaccurate statements regarding the amount of commissions, markup, or markdown**—There are circumstances where the amount of commission or markup may be higher than normal. That is permissible, as long as it is disclosed properly. However, telling a client that it costs him nothing to trade with your firm because you never charge a commission, and not informing him that all trades are done on a principal basis with a markup or markdown, is fraud.

TEST TOPIC ALERT   It is important to understand that, other than in the above circumstance where commissions may be higher than normal, a broker/dealer is not obligated to disclose the amount of commission on any offer to sell before the transaction. However, commissions are always required to be disclosed on the trade confirmation.

- **Stating or implying that the agent has inside information when such is not the case**—As we will see shortly, the use of non-public material *inside* information is a fraudulent practice. But, what about the agent who attempts to boost her credibility to clients by inferring that what she is about to tell them is "inside info" and, once released, will have a major impact on the stock? Since it isn't true, she isn't acting on inside information, but, she is still guilty of making untrue statements.

- **Telling a customer that a security will be listed on an exchange without concrete information concerning its listing statue**—Years ago, before the Nasdaq Stock Market became the home for so many leading companies, an announcement that a stock was going to be listed on the NYSE invariably caused its market price to jump. Even though it does not have the same significance today, any statement of this type relating to a change in marketplace for the security is only permitted if, in fact, you have knowledge that such change is imminent.

- **Informing a client that the registration of a security with the SEC or with the state securities Administrator means that the security has been approved by these regulators**—Registration never implies approval.

- **Misrepresenting the status of customer accounts**—This behavior is fraudulent. Many people are not motivated to pay strict attention to their monthly account statements, making it relatively easy for an unscrupulous agent to fraudulently claim increasing values in the account when the opposite is true. Doing so would be a fraudulent action.

- **Promising a customer services without any intent to perform them or without being properly qualified to perform them**—You say, "Yes, I can" to your client, even if you know you cannot deliver. For instance, the client asks you to analyze his bond portfolio to determine the average duration. Even though you do not know how to do that, you agree to do so. Under the USA, you committed fraud.

- **Representing to customers that the Administrator approves of the broker/dealer's or agent's abilities**—This is another case of using the word *approve* improperly. A broker/dealer or agent is registered, not approved.

TEST TOPIC ALERT

Merely learning the terms is not enough to get you through the exam. On the exam, you must be able to identify situations in which the above violations occur. Be able to apply the concepts of fraud and unethical behavior to scenarios that are likely to occur in everyday business.

CASE STUDY

Making Leading or Untrue Statements

Situation: Mr. Thompson, a registered securities agent in Illinois, informs a long-standing client, Ms. Gordon, that her largest equity holding, First Tech Internet Services, Inc., will be listed on the NYSE upon completion of its application for listing. In addition, he exaggerates the earnings by $1 per share to make her more comfortable and encourage her to buy more shares. Mr. Thompson is convinced the earnings will rise to that amount and does not want Ms. Gordon to sell because he believes the stock will appreciate in price once listed on the Exchange. He also tells her that his firm will not be charging her any commission on the trade as they already have the stock in inventory, so she will be ahead from the start.

Analysis: Mr. Thompson violated the USA by deliberately misrepresenting the earnings of First Tech Internet Services. Although Mr. Thompson's motives may have been good, he must be truthful in his effort to encourage clients to purchase more stock—his conviction that the stock would rise upon its listing on the NYSE is not sufficient. No violation of the act occurred with respect to First Tech's Exchange listing because Mr. Thompson knew that the stock had a pending application to be listed on the NYSE. To state that she will be ahead from the start because the firm will not charge a commission, but failing to state that a sale from inventory would include a markup, is a fraudulent act.

4. 1. 1. 2   Failure to State Material Facts

The USA does not require an agent to provide all information about an investment, but only information that is material to making an informed investment decision. However, the agent must not fail to mention material information that could affect the price of the security. In addition, the agent may not state facts that in and of themselves are true but, as a result of deliberately omitting other facts, render the recommendation misleading under the circumstances.

TEST TOPIC ALERT

Full disclosure also applies when filling out an order to purchase or sell securities, referred to as an order ticket. Each order ticket must disclose the account ID, a description of the security including the number of shares if a stock and total par value if a bond, the terms and conditions of the order (market or limit), the time of order entry and execution, the execution price, and the identity of the agent who accepted the order or is responsible for the account. We do not need the client's name or address on the order ticket.

CASE STUDY

Failure to State Material Facts

Situation: Upon NYSE acceptance of the listing application, there is an announcement that First Tech Internet Services will publish its financial statements in a newspaper advertisement. Mr. Thompson deliberately failed to mention this advertisement to Ms. Gordon.

After its listing on the NYSE, the research department in Mr. Thompson's firm prepares a negative report on First Tech. The research department discovered a change in accounting practices that will have a detrimental effect on subsequent earnings reported by First Tech. Mr. Thompson continues to recommend the stock to Ms. Gordon because he believes the increased exposure gained by the Exchange listing will outweigh the future decline in earnings. As a result, Mr. Thompson neglects to inform Ms. Gordon of the change before her purchase of additional shares.

Analysis: Mr. Thompson violated the USA even though he made no misleading statements to Ms. Gordon with respect to First Tech. Mr. Thompson did not have to mention the advertisement in the newspaper because it is not material, yet he violated the act when he failed to mention the accounting change that would result in significantly lower earnings. Although an accounting change is not ordinarily a material fact, in this case it was because it would have a detrimental impact on the company's earnings and its market price. An informed investor must have such information.

4. 1. 1. 3   Using Inside Information

Making recommendations on the basis of material inside information about an issuer or its securities is prohibited. Should an agent come into possession of inside information, the agent must report the possession of the information to a supervisor or compliance officer. However, the use of a broker/dealer or investment adviser's internally generated research report prior to public release is not considered use of inside information.

TAKE NOTE

Material inside information under securities law is any information about a company that has not been communicated to the general public and that would likely affect the value of a security. Even if you acquire the information "accidentally," you cannot use it until it becomes public.

TEST TOPIC ALERT

The exam may ask you to identify who is guilty of insider trading violations—a corporate officer of the issuer who divulges material inside information to a friend, but no transaction takes place, or an agent who executes a trade for a client who is acting on inside information? Simply giving someone inside information, although imprudent, is not a violation of the law. Only when the information is used for trading does a violation occur. In our question, the agent is in violation for accepting an order on the basis of material nonpublic information that results in a trade.

CASE STUDY

Using Inside Information

Situation: Mr. Thompson is a friend and neighbor of Mr. Cage, president and owner of more than half of First Tech's securities. Mr. Cage discloses to Mr. Thompson that the company has just discovered a new technology that will double First Tech's earnings within the next year. No one outside of the company, except for Mr. Thompson, knows of this discovery. On this basis, Mr. Thompson buys additional shares of First Tech for Ms. Gordon.

Analysis: The information on First Tech's new technology is material inside information that has not been made public. It is material information that only Mr. Thompson and company officials know. Mr. Thompson violated the USA by acting on this information. Mr. Thompson should have communicated the possession of the information to his compliance officer and refrained from making recommendations on the basis of this information.

4. 2 DISHONEST AND UNETHICAL BUSINESS PRACTICES OF BROKER/DEALERS AND AGENTS

In 1983, NASAA released a Statement of Policy enumerating a large number of business practices that, when engaged in by broker/dealers or agents, they deemed dishonest or unethical. Subsequently, they have issued several Model Rules that have expanded the list. Most students report seeing at least a dozen questions on their Series 63 exam that are drawn from the following material, especially those relating uniquely to agents. In most cases, the listed prohibition is logical common sense, "don't lie, don't cheat, and don't steal". However, due to the nature of this exam and their legal interpretations, particularly for those of you without a securities or law background, further explanations will be supplied.

The premise of the Policy is that each broker/dealer and agent shall observe high standards of commercial honor and just and equitable principles of trade in the conduct of their business. Acts and practices, including but not limited to those enumerated below, are considered contrary to such standards and may constitute grounds for denial, suspension or revocation of registration or such other action authorized by the Uniform Securities Act. You will need to know that it is a dishonest or unethical business practice if a broker/dealer is doing any of the following (those that apply to agents as well are marked with an *).

4. 2. 1   DELIVERY DELAYS

Engaging in a pattern of unreasonable and unjustifiable delays in the delivery of securities purchased by any of its customers and/or in the payment upon request of free credit balances reflecting completed transactions of any of its customers. A free credit balance is just like a credit balance on your charge card—it is your money and must be sent to you upon request. In the event that the client requests a certificate for the security purchased, it would be considered an unethical business practice for the firm to delay delivering it to the client.

4. 2. 2   CHURNING*

Inducing trading in a customer's account which is excessive in size or frequency in view of the financial resources, objectives, and character of the account. A key here is the word *excessive*. By definition, anytime something is excessive, it is too much. The regulators understand that different clients have different needs and ability to take risks, so what is excessive for the 80-year-old pensioner is probably not going to be so for the 40-year-old partner in a major law firm.

4. 2. 3   UNSUITABLE RECOMMENDATIONS*

Recommending to a customer the purchase, sale, or exchange of any security without reasonable grounds to believe that such transaction or recommendation is suitable for the customer based upon reasonable inquiry concerning the customer's investment objectives, financial situation and needs, and any other relevant information known by the broker/dealer.

Agents must always have reasonable grounds for making recommendations to clients. Before making recommendations, the agent must inquire into the client's financial status, investment objectives, and ability to assume financial risk. What about the client who refuses to give any financial information or discuss objectives? In that case, all the agent can do is accept unsolicited orders because there is no basis for making any recommendation.

The following practices violate the suitability requirements under the USA as well as the rules of fair practice that regulatory agencies have developed. A securities professional may not:

- recommend securities transactions without regard to the customer's financial situation, needs, or investment objectives;
- induce transactions solely to generate commissions (**churning**), defined as transactions in customer accounts that are excessive in size or frequency in relation to the client's financial resources, objectives, or the character of the account;
- recommend a security without reasonable grounds;
- make blanket recommendations. That is, it will almost always be unsuitable if the same security is recommended to the majority of your clients. How could all of them have the

same needs? Some are looking for income, some for growth, and some for safety, and no one security can provide all three; and

■ fail to sufficiently describe the important facts and risks concerning a transaction or security.

CASE STUDY   **Making Unsuitable Investment Recommendations**

Situation: Mr. Thompson has a wide variety of clients: high-net-worth individuals, trusts, retirees with limited incomes and resources, and college students. Mr. Thompson has strong beliefs about First Tech, a growth stock that pays no dividends. He aggressively recommends the stock to all his clients without informing them of the volatility of First Tech and the the firm's research department's pending downgrade in earnings.

Analysis: Mr. Thompson has violated the USA on several counts. First, he made a recommendation without regard to the separate financial conditions, needs, and objectives of his diverse client base. The recommendation is unsuitable for the investment objectives of his retired clients with fixed incomes and limited financial resources. In addition, he made the recommendation in an unsuitable manner by failing to reveal the earnings volatility or risk and the downgrade in earnings.

4. 2. 4   UNAUTHORIZED TRANSACTIONS*

Executing a transaction on behalf of a customer without authorization to do so. Unless discretionary authorization (see following) has been received, broker/dealers and their agents may never enter an order for a client on their own volition, even when it is in the best interest of the client. You may be asked a question where a spouse of a client or other person with a strong personal relationship contacts the agent with transaction instructions, allegedly on behalf of the client. Unless there is a written third-party trading authorization on file, no activity can take place.

Somewhat related to this activity is deliberately failing to follow a customer's instructions. In this case, the client has given the terms of the order and if the agent decides to purchase more or less than ordered, or in any other way change the nature of the order, it is a prohibited practice.

4. 2. 5   EXERCISING DISCRETION*

Exercising any discretionary power in effecting a transaction for a customer's account without first obtaining written discretionary authority from the customer, unless the discretionary power relates solely to the time and/or price for the executing of orders.

Agents of broker/dealers may not exercise discretion in an account without prior written authority (power of attorney) from the client. Prior written authority is also known as trading authorization.

Discretion is given to an agent by the client when the client authorizes (in writing) the agent to act on his own and use his discretion in deciding the following for the client:

■ Asset (security)

- Action (buy or sell)

- Amount (how many shares)

However, merely authorizing an agent to determine the best price or time to trade a security is not considered to be discretion.

CASE STUDY   **Discretionary Trading Authorization**

> **Situation:** Mr. Thompson's client, Mr. Bixby, has indicated over the phone that he authorizes Mr. Thompson to make trades for him. Mr. Bixby's family lawyer, Mr. Derval, has specific power of attorney over some of Mr. Bixby's businesses. Mr. Bixby promised Mr. Thompson that he would send in the trading authorization within the next day or two to give Mr. Thompson discretion over the account. However, Mr. Thompson immediately executed trades in First Tech for Mr. Bixby to take advantage of its impending NYSE listing.
>
> The following week, Mr. Thompson received Mr. Bixby's written discretionary trading authorization. On the day after the authorization arrived, Mr. Bixby's attorney, Mr. Derval, indicated that Mr. Bixby would like to buy shares in General Electric. Because Mr. Derval has power of attorney for Mr. Bixby, Mr. Thompson bought the shares.
>
> **Analysis:** Mr. Thompson violated the USA by trading in Mr. Bixby's account before receipt of the written trading authorization. Having authorization in the mail is not sufficient. Mr. Thompson also violated the USA by accepting the order from Mr. Derval because although he is Mr. Bixby's attorney, he was not specifically authorized to trade in Mr. Bixby's securities account. The trading authorization signed by Mr. Bixby only gave authority to Mr. Thompson. Had Mr. Derval provided Mr. Thompson with specific written third-party trading authorization from Mr. Bixby, Mr. Thompson then could have accepted the order for General Electric without a violation of the act.

---

4. 2. 6   MARGIN DOCUMENTS*

Executing any transaction in a margin account without securing from the customer a properly executed written margin agreement promptly *after* the initial transaction in the account.

4. 2. 7   COMMINGLING OF CUSTOMER AND FIRM ASSETS

Failing to segregate customers' free securities or securities held in safekeeping. Customer "free" securities are those which have no lien against them (just like one might have a lien against your car). Securities are pledged as collateral in a margin account.

Securities that are held in a customer's name must not be **commingled** (mixed) with securities of the firm.

If a firm has 100,000 shares of General Electric stock in its own proprietary account and its clients separately own an additional 100,000 shares, the firm may not place customer shares in the firm's proprietary account.

To mix shares together would give undue leverage or borrowing power to a firm and could jeopardize the security of client securities in the event of default.

One area of particular concern is brokerage firms maintaining margin accounts for their clients. In a margin account, the broker/dealer extends credit for the purchase of eligible securities and then uses those securities as collateral for the margin debt (loan). The pledging of these margin securities is known as **hypothecation**. There are strict rules regarding how much of the client's securities may be hypothecated and requiring that the balance be segregated from the firm's own securities.

4. 2. 8   IMPROPER HYPOTHECATION

Hypothecating a customer's securities without having a lien thereon unless the broker/dealer secures from the customer a properly executed written consent promptly after the initial transaction, except as permitted by rules of the Securities and Exchange Commission. As indicated previously, there are strict rules to be followed, the details of which will not be tested.

4. 2. 9   UNREASONABLE COMMISSIONS OR MARKUPS*

Entering into a transaction with or for a customer at a price not reasonably related to the current market price of the security or receiving an unreasonable commission or profit.

There is one way that a broker/dealer might make a very large profit and it would *not* be considered unreasonable. When acting in a dealer (or principal) capacity, broker/dealers sell out of inventory. What would be the situation if a firm bought some securities for their inventory and, several months later, the value of those securities had doubled or tripled? What would be a fair price to charge customers? The rules make it clear that quotes are always based on the current market so, in this case, the broker/dealer would make a substantial profit. By the way, this "sword cuts both ways." If the firm had stock in inventory that decreased greatly in value, the firm would not be able to pass any of the loss to clients—any sales would take place based on the current depressed market prices.

4. 2. 10   TIMELY PROSPECTUS DELIVERY*

Failing to furnish to a customer purchasing securities in an offering, no later than the due date of confirmation of the transaction, either a final prospectus or a preliminary prospectus.

Here is further detail from the USA that might answer a question on the exam: The Administrator may, by rule or order, require as a condition of registration under Coordination, that a prospectus be sent or given to each person to whom an offer is made no later than with confirmation of the trade. Of course, one must always be sent to a person who actually purchases the security. The Administrator may require that a prospectus for a security registered under Qualification be sent or given to each person to whom an offer is prior to the sale of the security rather than prior to the offer.

4. 2. 11   UNREASONABLE SERVICING FEES

Charging unreasonable and inequitable fees for services performed, including miscellaneous services such as collection of monies due for principal, dividends or interest, exchange or transfer of securities, appraisals, safekeeping, or custody of securities and other services related to its securities business. However, as long as these charges are not unreasonable, they would be permitted for performing these services.

4. 2. 12 DISHONORING QUOTES

Offering to buy from or sell to any person any security at a stated price unless such broker/dealer is prepared to purchase or sell, as the case may be, at such price and under such conditions as are stated at the time of such offer to buy or sell.

In other words, if a broker/dealer quotes a stock at 20.60 to 20.75, he had better be ready to sell at least the minimum trading unit (usually 100 shares) to a client at $20.75 per share (his ask or offering price), or buy from a client at $20.60 (his bid price).

4. 2. 13 MARKET MANIPULATION*

Effecting any transaction in, or inducing the purchase or sale of, any security by means of any manipulative, deceptive, or fraudulent device, practice, plan, program, design, or contrivance.

Securities legislation is designed to uphold the integrity of markets and transactions in securities. However, market integrity is violated when transactions misrepresent actual securities prices or market activity. The most common forms of market manipulation are matched orders and wash trades.

Matched orders occur when market participants agree to buy and sell securities among themselves to create the appearance of activity or trading in a security. Increased volume in a security can induce unsuspecting investors to purchase the security, thereby bidding up the price. As the price rises, participants who initiated the matched orders sell their securities at a profit.

A **wash trade** is an attempt to manipulate a security's price by creating an apparent interest in the security that really does not exist. This is done by an investor buying in one brokerage account and simultaneously selling through another. No real change in ownership has occurred, but to the marketplace, it appears that volume and/or price is increasing.

TAKE NOTE   **Arbitrage** is the simultaneous buying and selling of the same security in different markets to take advantage of different prices; it is not a form of market manipulation. Simultaneously buying a security in one market and selling it in another forces prices to converge and, therefore, provides uniform prices for the general public.

4. 2. 14 GUARANTEEING AGAINST LOSS*

Guaranteeing a customer against loss in any securities account of such customer carried by the broker/dealer or in any securities transaction effected by the broker/dealer or in any securities transaction effected by the broker/dealer with or for such customer.

Securities professionals may not guarantee a certain performance, nor may they guarantee against a loss by providing funds to the account.

TEST TOPIC ALERT   The term *guaranteed* under the USA means "guaranteed as to payment of principal, interest, or dividends." It is allowable to refer to a guaranteed security when an entity other than the issuer is making the guarantee. However, the regulatory agencies of the securities industry prohibit securities professionals from guaranteeing the performance returns of an investment or portfolio.

4. 2. 15 DISSEMINATING FALSE TRADING INFORMATION*

Publishing or circulating, or causing to be published or circulated, any notice, circular, advertisement, newspaper article, investment service, or communication of any kind which purports to report any transaction as a purchase or sale of any security unless such broker/dealer believes that such transaction was a bona fide purchase or sale or such security; or which purports to quote the bid price or asked price for any security, unless such broker/dealer believes that such quotation represents a bona fide bid for, or offer of, such security.

4. 2. 16 DECEPTIVE ADVERTISING PRACTICES*

Using any advertising or sales presentation in such a fashion as to be deceptive or misleading. An example of such practice would be a distribution of any nonfactual data, material or presentation based on conjecture, unfounded or unrealistic claims or assertions in any brochure, flyer, or display by words, pictures, graphs, or otherwise designed to supplement, detract from, supersede, or defeat the purpose or effect of any prospectus or disclosure.

One way in which this violation occurs is when a broker/dealer or agent prepares a sales brochure for a new issue but includes only the positive information from the prospectus. Leaving out risk factors and other potential "deal-killing" information is prohibited. Somewhat related, and also prohibited, is **highlighting** or making any other marks on a prospectus to draw attention to key points.

4. 2. 17 FAILING TO DISCLOSE CONFLICTS OF INTEREST

Failing to disclose that the broker/dealer is controlled by, controlling, affiliated with or under common control with the issuer of any security before entering into any contract with or for a customer for the purchase or sale of such security, the existence of such control to such customer, and if such disclosure is not made in writing, it shall be supplemented by the giving or sending of written disclosure at or before the completion of the transaction.

Suppose you were selling shares of a company where your sister was a control person? Do you think you'd have to disclose that potential conflict to your clients? Yes!

4. 2. 18 WITHHOLDING SHARES OF A PUBLIC OFFERING

Failing to make a bona fide public offering of all of the securities allotted to a broker/dealer for distribution, whether acquired as an underwriter, a selling group member, or from a member participating in the distribution as an underwriter or selling group member. If the firm is fortunate to be part of the underwriting of one of these IPOs that rockets in price because the issue is *oversubscribed*, they better be sure to allocate the shares to clients in an equitable manner and not keep any for themselves.

4. 2. 19   RESPONDING TO COMPLAINTS*

Failure or refusal to furnish a customer, upon reasonable request, information to which he is entitled, or to respond to a formal written request or complaint.

When a written complaint is received by the firm (and only written complaints are recognized), action must be taken. The complainant (customer) would be notified that the complaint had been received and an entry would be made in the firm's complaint file. If an agent were the subject of the complaint, the agent would be notified, but would *not* be given a copy of the complaint (agents do not have recordkeeping requirements). If the complaint is received by the agent rather than the firm, the agent must report the complaint to the appropriate supervisor. In the unusual case (except on the exam) where a customer files a written complaint and then withdraws it, the firm makes a copy of the communication, places it in their complaint file, and then returns the original to the client. If the complaint is sent by email, that is considered *in writing*.

4. 2. 20   FRONT RUNNING*

Front running is the unethical business practice of a broker/dealer or one of its representatives placing a personal order ahead of a previously received customer order. It occurs most frequently when the firm has received an institutional order of sufficient size to move the market. By running in front of the order, the firm or representative can profit on that movement.

CASE STUDY   **Practices—Customer Complaints and Front Running**

Situation: Mr. Thompson, an agent with First Securities, a broker/dealer, recommends to his client, Mr. Byers, that he purchase ABC Shoe Co., a thinly traded chain store that First Securities's analysts have highly recommended subsequent to its initial public offering. Mr. Byers agrees. Just before entering Mr. Byers's order, Mr. Thompson purchases several hundred shares for himself. Mr. Byers learned of Mr. Thompson's purchase and wrote him a stinging letter of complaint about it. Because Mr. Thompson considered the transaction a private matter, he did not think it necessary to bring the letter to the attention of First Securities. A few days later, Mr. Thompson personally apologized to Mr. Byers and took him out for a drink.

Analysis: Mr. Thompson has engaged in two practices that violate industry practice. First, although the recommendation of ABC Shoe Co. was perfectly appropriate, it was not appropriate for Mr. Thompson to enter his personal order for the same shares before completing Mr. Byers's purchase. This is known as front running, a prohibited practice. Additionally, Mr. Thompson (as a registered agent) must bring all written complaints to the attention of his employer. Had Mr. Byers simply lodged an oral complaint, Mr. Thompson would not have been under an obligation to bring it to the attention of the manager of his office. Taking Mr. Byers out for a drink did not violate industry standards.

4. 2. 21 SPREADING RUMORS*

Any agent hearing a rumor must report it to the appropriate supervisor. Broker/dealers must insure that rumors they become aware of are not spread or used in any way, particularly not as the basis for recommendations.

4. 2. 22 BACKDATING RECORDS*

All records and documents must reflect their actual dates. Although there can be tax or other benefits to clients when their trade confirmations are backdated, it is an unethical business practice to do so.

4. 2. 23 WAIVERS

The USA makes it clear that any condition, stipulation, or provision binding any person acquiring any security or receiving any investment advice to waive compliance with any provision of the Act or any rule or order hereunder is void. For exam purposes, if you are given a question where clients agree to waive their rights to sue, the agreement is null and void.

4. 2. 24 INVESTMENT COMPANY SALES*

In 1997, NASAA adopted the NASAA Statement of Policy titled Dishonest or Unethical Business Practices by Broker-Dealers and Agents in Connection with Investment Company Shares. Several of those items are currently being tested. Under this Policy, any broker/dealer or agent who engages in one or more of the following practices shall be deemed to have engaged in "dishonest or unethical practices in the securities business" as used in the Uniform Securities Act, and such conduct may constitute grounds for denial, suspension, or revocation of registration or such other action authorized by statute.

4. 2. 24. 1 Sales Load Communications

In connection with the solicitation of investment company shares, stating or implying to a customer that the shares are sold without a commission, are "no load" or have "no sales charge" if there is associated with the purchase of the shares:
- a front-end load;
- a contingent deferred sales load (CDSC); or
- a Rule 12b-1 fee or a service fee if such fees in total exceed .25% of average net fund assets per year.

4. 2. 24. 2 Breakpoints

In connection with the solicitation of investment company shares, failing to disclose to any customer any relevant:
- sales charge discount on the purchase of shares in dollar amounts at or above a breakpoint; or
- letter of intent feature, if available, which will reduce the sales charges.

4. 2. 24. 3 Unfair Comparisons

It is considered an unethical business practice to compare or in any way imply that money market mutual funds are similar to savings accounts at insured banks. Although generally quite safe, money market funds do not have FDIC insurance and there is no guarantee that their principal will not fluctuate.

4. 2. 25 PRACTICES RELATING SOLELY TO AGENTS

4. 2. 25. 1 Lending or Borrowing

Engaging in the practice of lending to or borrowing money or securities from a customer. Securities professionals may not borrow money or securities from a client unless the client is a broker/dealer, an affiliate of the professional, or a financial institution engaged in the business of loaning money.

Securities professionals may not loan money to clients unless the firm is a broker/dealer or financial institution engaged in the business of loaning funds or the client is an affiliate.

C A S E S T U D Y   **Borrowing Money or Securities from Clients**

> **Situation:** On occasion, Mr. Thompson borrows cash from his discretionary client, Mr. Bixby, when Mr. Bixby's account is not fully invested. Mr. Bixby has given Mr. Thompson much latitude because Mr. Thompson has done well in managing the account and Mr. Thompson always repays the money in time to reinvest Mr. Bixby's funds in new securities purchases. Mr. Thompson justifies these borrowings as within the discretionary power Mr. Bixby had granted him. The First National Bank is also a client of Mr. Thompson, but he does not borrow from the bank because it charges unusually high interest rates.
>
> **Analysis:** Mr. Thompson has engaged in a prohibited practice because securities professionals may not borrow from customers who are not in the business of lending money. Furthermore, Mr. Thompson violated the USA in exceeding the specific discretionary authority that Mr. Bixby had authorized. Mr. Bixby had authorized Mr. Thompson to trade in securities—not to take his money for personal use. Had Mr. Thompson decided to borrow from The First National Bank, it would have been permitted because it is an entity engaged in the business of lending money.

T E S T T O P I C A L E R T

> As a former President of the United States once said, "Let me make one thing perfectly clear." When it comes to borrowing or lending money, you cannot borrow from *any* client (including your mother), unless that client is a lending institution such as a bank or credit union. Likewise, as an agent, you can never lend money to any client unless the client has some kind of affiliation with your firm. If your broker/dealer handles margin accounts, then, of course, money can be loaned to clients. Don't take this personally, just get the questions right on the exam.

4. 2. 25. 2 Selling Away

Effecting securities transactions not recorded on the regular books or records of the broker/dealer which the agent represents, unless the transactions are authorized in writing by the broker/dealer prior to execution of the transaction.

CASE STUDY

Practices—Trades Not on the Books

Situation: Mr. Thompson, a registered agent for First Securities, Inc., of Illinois, is also a part owner of Computer Resources, Inc., a privately held company in the state. Mr. Thompson is also a friend of Mr. Byers, the chairman of Aircraft Parts, Inc., a large manufacturing company traded on the NYSE. Mr. Byers has an account with Mr. Thompson at First Securities.

Mr. Thompson decides to sell his shares in Computer Resources to one of his clients. Because the shares are not publicly traded, Mr. Thompson completes the trades without informing First Securities or recording the transaction on their books. Mr. Thompson believes there is no need to inform his employer because the transaction was private. On the following day, Mr. Byers calls Mr. Thompson and indicates that he would like to sell his shares in Aircraft Parts. Mr. Thompson, who now has plenty of liquid assets from the sale of his shares in Computer Resources, decides to buy the shares directly from Mr. Byers. Mr. Thompson does not record the trade on the records of First Securities because he considers it a private transaction between himself and Mr. Byers.

Analysis: In both cases, Mr. Thompson has engaged in a prohibited practice. A registered agent may not conduct transactions with customers of his employing broker/dealer that are not recorded on the books without prior written consent. It makes no difference whether the shares Mr. Thompson sold were privately held; when an agent effects trades with clients of the firm, the transactions must be recorded on the books of the firm unless prior written authorization is obtained from the firm.

TEST TOPIC ALERT

The exam may refer to this as a trade made off the books of the broker/dealer. Just remember that it is considered to be a prohibited practice anytime an agent effects securities transactions not recorded on the regular books or records of the broker/dealer the agent represents, unless the transactions are authorized in writing by the broker/dealer before execution of the transaction.

4. 2. 25. 3 Fictitious Accounts

Establishing or maintaining an account containing fictitious information in order to execute transactions which would otherwise be prohibited. Examples of this kind of conduct sometimes given on the exam are "beefing up" a client's net worth to enable him to engage in margin or options trading, or making him appear to have more investment experience than is true.

4. 2. 25. 4 Sharing in Accounts

Sharing directly or indirectly in profits or losses in the account of any customer without the written authorization of the customer and the broker/dealer which the agent represents.

Agents cannot share in the profits or losses of client accounts unless the client and the broker/dealer supply prior written approval. In such a situation, it would be permissible to commingle the agent's and the customer's funds because they have a joint account.

TEST TOPIC ALERT

Unlike agents, broker/dealers, investment advisers, and investment adviser representatives are never permitted to share in the profits or losses in their client's accounts.

4. 2. 25. 5 Splitting Commissions

Dividing or otherwise splitting the agent's commissions, profits, or other compensation from the purchase or sale of securities with any person not also registered as an agent for the same broker/dealer, or for a broker/dealer under direct or indirect common control. It is not necessary to disclose to an agent's client that he is splitting commissions with another agent *unless* it increases the transaction cost to the client.

QUICK QUIZ 4.A

Write **U** for unlawful or prohibited activities and **L** for lawful activities.

_____ 1. An agent guarantees a client that funds invested in mutual funds made up of government securities cannot lose principal.

_____ 2. A nondiscretionary customer calls his agent and places a buy order for 1,000 shares of any hot Internet company. Later in the day, the agent enters an order for 1,000 shares of Global Internet Services.

_____ 3. An agent receives a call from his client's spouse, advising him to sell her husband's securities. Her husband is out of the country and requested that his wife call the agent. The agent refuses because the wife does not have trading authorization, and she complains vigorously to his manager.

_____ 4. A client writes a letter of complaint to his agent regarding securities that the agent had recommended. The agent calls the client to apologize and then disposes of the letter because the client seemed satisfied.

_____ 5. A registered agent borrows $10,000 from a credit union that is one of her best customers.

_____ 6. An agent is convinced that Internet Resources will rise significantly over the next 3 months. She offers to buy the stock back from her customers at 10% higher than its current price at any time during the next 3 months.

_____ 7. An agent receives an order for the purchase of an obscure foreign security. The agent informs the client that the commissions and charges on this purchase will be much higher than those of domestic securities.

_____   8.   An agent who works for a small broker/dealer that employs no securities analysts assures her clients that she can analyze any publicly traded security better than any analyst and that she will do it personally for each security purchased by a client, regardless of the industry.

_____   9.   An agent recommends that her client buy 1,000 shares of Internet Consultants, Inc., an unregistered nonexempt security with a bright future.

Quick Quiz answers can be found at the end of the Unit.

4. 3 UNETHICAL BUSINESS PRACTICES OF INVESTMENT ADVISERS

The fraudulent and prohibited practices described in the previous section relate to the sale of securities. The USA also prohibits fraudulent and unethical activities by persons providing investment advice.

The USA makes it unlawful for any person who receives compensation (directly or indirectly) for advising another person (whether through analyses or reports) on the value of securities to use any device, scheme, or artifice to defraud the other person. Additionally, that person may not engage in any act, practice, or course of business that operates or would operate as fraud or deceit upon the other person or engage in dishonest or unethical practices as the Administrator may define by rule.

We will list in the following those items which are included in NASAA's Statement of Policy—Unethical Business Practices of Investment Advisers. Following each one, we have included NASAA's review notes giving an explanation of the prohibition. They derive the exam questions from these notes, so please study them. You can expect about six questions from this topic on your Series 63 exam.

Although many of the activities listed in the following are similar to those prohibited to broker/dealers and agents, the fiduciary responsibility that an investment adviser possesses pervades everything that advisers do. While the extent and nature of this duty varies according to the nature of the relationship between and investment adviser (or IAR) and their clients and the circumstances of each case, an investment adviser shall not engage in unethical business practices as enumerated in the following sections.

TAKE NOTE   Prohibitions are determined by the nature of the activity, not the registration status of the person engaged in the activity. Broker/dealers and their agents may give investment advice, yet not be included in the definition of investment adviser. Nevertheless, they are subject to the antifraud provisions of the act when they do provide advice. Why? The antifraud provisions of the USA refer to "any person" who commits fraud when selling securities or when providing investment advice with respect to securities.

4. 3. 1   SUITABILITY OF RECOMMENDATIONS

Recommending to a client to whom investment supervisory, management, or consulting services are provided the purchase, sale, or exchange of any security without reasonable grounds to believe that the recommendation is suitable for the client on the basis of information furnished by the client after reasonable inquiry concerning the client's investment objectives, financial situation, and needs, and any other information known by the investment adviser.

Review Note: An investment adviser providing investment supervisory, management, or consulting services has a fundamental obligation to analyze a client's financial situation and needs prior to making any recommendation to the client. Recommendations made to a client must be reasonable in relation to the information that is obtained concerning the client's investment objective, financial situation, and needs, and other information known by the investment adviser. By failing to make reasonable inquiry or by failing to make recommendations that are in line with the financial situation, investment objectives, and character of a client's account, an investment adviser has not met its primary responsibility.

TAKE NOTE   What about the client who refuses to give any financial information or discuss objectives? In that case, the investment adviser will probably refuse to do business with the person. This is different than the same scenario with an agent. An agent's only job is to effect securities transactions, while that of the IA or IAR is to give advice—its part of that fiduciary responsibility. How can you possibly give advice if you have no idea what would be appropriate for the client?

TEST TOPIC ALERT   It is possible you might have a test question where the investment adviser (or IAR) recommends the same security to most or all of their customers. This would generally be a prohibited practice because it is highly unlikely that the same security would be suitable for all clients. This could also be referred to as *blanket recommendations*.

4. 3. 2   DISCRETIONARY POWERS

Exercising any discretionary power in placing an order for the purchase or sale of securities for a client without obtaining prior written discretionary authority from the client, unless the discretionary power relates solely to the price at which, or the time when, an order involving a definite amount of a specified security shall be executed, or both.

Review Note: This rule pertains only to investment advisers that place orders for client accounts. Prior to placing an order for an account, an investment adviser exercising discretion should have written discretionary authority from the client. In most cases, discretionary authority is granted in an advisory contract or in a separate document executed at the time the contract is executed. The rule permits oral discretionary authority to be used for the initial transactions in a customer's account within the first 10 business days after the date of the first transaction. Please note that this policy differs from that for broker/dealers and agents (who must receive written authorization prior to the first discretionary trade). An investment adviser is not precluded from exercising discretionary power that relates solely to the price or time at which an order involving a specific amount of a security is authorized by a customer because time and price do not constitute discretion.

4. 3. 3   EXCESSIVE TRADING

Inducing trading in a client's account that is excessive in size or frequency in view of the financial resources, investment objectives, and character of the account.

Review Note: This rule is intended to prevent an excessive number of securities transactions from being induced by an investment adviser. There are many situations where an investment adviser may receive commissions, or be affiliated with a person that receives commissions, from the securities transactions that are placed by the investment adviser. In view of the fact that an adviser in such situations can directly benefit from the number of securities transactions effected in a client's account, the rule appropriately forbids an excessive number of transaction orders to be induced by an adviser for a customer's account.

4. 3. 4   UNAUTHORIZED TRADING

Placing an order to purchase or sell a security for the account of a client without authority to do so.

Review Note: This rule is not new to either the securities or investment advisory professions. An investment adviser must have authority to place any order for the account of a client. The authority may be obtained from a client orally or in an agreement executed by the client giving the adviser blanket authority.

4. 3. 5   THIRD PARTY TRADING

Placing an order to purchase or sell a security for the account of a client upon instruction of a third party without first having obtained a written third-party trading authorization from the client.

Review Note: It is sound business practice for an investment adviser not to place an order for the account of a customer on instruction of a third party without first knowing that the third party has obtained authority from the client for the order. For example, it would be important for an investment adviser to know that an attorney had power of attorney over an estate whose securities the adviser was managing prior to placing any order on instruction of the attorney. Placing orders under such circumstances could result in substantial civil liability, besides being an unethical practice.

4. 3. 6   BORROWING FROM CLIENTS

Borrowing money or securities from a client unless the client is a broker/dealer, an affiliate of the investment adviser, or financial institution engaged in the business of loaning funds.

Review Note: Unless a client of an investment adviser is engaged in the business of loaning money, is an affiliate of the investment adviser, or is an institution that would engage in this type of activity, an investment adviser must not take advantage of its advisory role by borrowing funds from a client. A client provides a substantial amount of confidential information to an investment adviser regarding the client's financial situation and needs. Using that information to an investment adviser's own advantage by borrowing funds is a breach of confidentiality and may create a material conflict of interest that could influence the advice rendered by the adviser to the client.

4. 3. 7 LENDING TO CLIENTS

Loaning money to a client unless the investment adviser is a financial institution engaged in the business of loaning funds or the client is an affiliate of the investment adviser.

Review Note: Like borrowing money from a client, loaning funds to a client by an investment adviser should not be an allowable practice unless the investment adviser is a financial institution normally engaged in the business of loaning funds or unless the client is affiliated with the adviser. Loaning funds may influence decisions made for a client's account and puts the investment adviser in a conflict of interest position because the client becomes a debtor of the adviser after a loan is made.

4. 3. 8 MISREPRESENTING QUALIFICATIONS

To misrepresent to any advisory client, or prospective advisory client, the qualifications of the investment adviser or any employee of the investment adviser, or to misrepresent the nature of the advisory services being offered or fees to be charged for such service, or to omit to state a material fact necessary to make the statements made regarding qualifications, services or fees, in light of the circumstances under which they are made, not misleading.

Review Note: When an investment adviser offers its services to a prospective client or when providing services to an existing client, the qualifications of the investment adviser or any employee of the investment adviser and the nature of the advisory services and the fees to be charged must be disclosed in such a way as to not mislead. Overstating the qualifications of the investment adviser or disclosing inaccurately the nature of the advisory services to be provided or fees to be charged are not ethical ways to either acquire or retain clients.

4. 3. 9 THIRD PARTY REPORTS OR RECOMMENDATIONS

Providing a report or recommendation to any advisory client prepared by someone other than the adviser without disclosing the fact. (This prohibition does not apply to a situation where the adviser uses published research reports or statistical analyses to render advice or where an adviser orders such a report in the normal course of providing service.)

Review Note: If an investment adviser provides a report to a client that is prepared by a third party, the adviser has a responsibility to disclose the fact to the client. By entering into an investment advisory agreement, the client relies upon the expertise of the adviser to provide the advisory service. Thus, if the advice is provided by a third party, it is imperative that the adviser disclose this fact to the client so the client is not misled. The prohibition does not apply when an investment adviser gathers and uses research materials prior to making its recommendation to a client.

4. 3. 10 UNREASONABLE ADVISORY FEES

Charging a client an unreasonable advisory fee.

Review Note: This rule is intended to prohibit an investment adviser from charging an excessively high advisory fee. *Unreasonable*, as used in this rule, means unreasonable in relation to fees charged by other advisers for similar services. Although no two advisory services are exactly alike, comparisons can be drawn. In those instances where an advisory fee is out of line with fees charged by other advisers providing essentially the same services, an investment adviser should justify the charge. It would be very difficult for a client to compare various advisory services to evaluate those services and the fees charged. This rule will allow state Administrators to research the competitiveness of an adviser's services and fees to make a determination as to whether the fees being charged are unreasonably high.

4. 3. 11   CONFLICTS OF INTEREST

Failing to disclose to clients in writing, before any advice is rendered, any material conflict of interest relating to the adviser or any of its employees which could reasonably be expected to impair the rendering of unbiased and objective advice including:

- compensation arrangements connected with advisory services to clients which are in addition to compensation from such clients for such services; and

- charging a client an advisory fee for rendering advice when a commission for executing securities transactions pursuant to such advice will be received by the adviser or its employees.

Review Note: This rule is designed to require disclosure of all material conflicts of interest relating to the adviser or any of its employees that could affect the advice that is rendered. The two examples cited in the rule pertain to compensation arrangements that benefit the adviser and that are connected with advisory services being provided. However, full disclosure of all other material conflicts of interest, such as affiliations between the investment adviser and product suppliers, are also required to be made under the rule.

4. 3. 12   GUARANTEEING RESULTS

Guaranteeing a client that a specific result will be achieved (gain or no loss) with advice which will be rendered.
Review Note: An investment adviser should not guarantee any gain or against loss in connection with advice that is rendered. By doing so, the adviser fails to maintain an arms-length relationship with a client and puts himself in a conflict of interest position by having a direct interest in the outcome of the advice rendered by the adviser.

4. 3. 13   ADVERTISING

Publishing, circulating, or distributing any advertisement which does not comply with the Investment Advisers Act of 1940.
Review Note: An investment adviser should not publish, circulate, or distribute any advertisement that is inconsistent with federal rules governing the use of advertisements. Rule 206(4)-1 of the Investment Advisers Act of 1940 contains prohibitions against advertisements containing untrue statements of material fact that refer directly or indirectly to any testimonial of any kind, that refer to past specific recommendations of the investment adviser unless certain conditions are met (such as including all recommendations, both winners and losers, for a period of at least the previous 12 months), that represent that a chart or formula or other device being offered can, by itself, be used to determine which securities are to be bought or sold, or that contain a statement that any analysis, report, or service will be furnished free

when such is not the case. These prohibitions are fundamental and sound standards that all investment advisers should follow.

An advertisement is defined as a communication to more than one person. For those of you have taken a FINRA exam, there is no differentiation between advertisement and sales literature. In addition, although the rules do not prohibit **testimonials** for broker/dealers, they are strictly forbidden for use by IAs. One thing to look for on the exam deals with investment advisers who advertise a charting or similar system—they must indicate that there are *limitations and difficulties* inherent in using such programs.

4. 3. 14   UNAUTHORIZED DISCLOSURES

Disclosing the identity, affairs, or investments of any client unless required by law to do so, or unless consented to by the client.

Review Note: An investment advisory firm has a responsibility to ensure that all information collected from a client be kept confidential. The only exception to the rule should be in instances where the client authorized the release of such information or when the investment advisory firm is required by law to disclose such information.

TAKE NOTE   If the account is a joint one, such as with a spouse, the adviser does not need consent to discuss account matters with either party.

4. 3. 15   IMPROPER CUSTODY

Taking any action, directly or indirectly, with respect to those securities or funds in which any client has any beneficial interest, where the investment adviser has custody or possession of such securities or funds when the adviser's action is subject to and does not comply with the requirements of the Investment Advisers Act of 1940.

Review Note: In instances where an investment adviser has custody or possession of client's funds or securities, it should comply with the regulations under the Investment Advisers Act of 1940 designed to ensure the safekeeping of those securities and funds. The rules under the act specifically provide that securities of clients be segregated and properly marked, that the funds of the clients be deposited in separate bank accounts, that the investment adviser notify each client as to the place and manner in which such funds and securities are being maintained, that an itemized list of all securities and funds in the adviser's possession be sent to the client not less frequently than every three months, and that all such funds and securities be verified annually by actual examination by an independent CPA on a surprise basis. The rule establishes very conservative measures to safeguard each client's funds and securities held by an investment adviser.

4. 3. 16   WRITTEN REQUIREMENT FOR CONTRACTS

Entering into, extending or renewing any investment advisory contract unless such contract is in *writing* and discloses, in substance, the services to be provided, the term of the contract, the advisory fee, the formula for computing the fee, the amount of prepaid fee to be returned in the event of contract termination or non-performance, whether the contract grants discretionary power to the adviser and that no assignment of such contract shall be made by the investment adviser without the consent of the other party to the contract.

Review Note: The purpose of this rule is to ensure that clients have a document to refer to that describes the basic terms of the agreement the client has entered into with an adviser.

4. 4 FIDUCIARY RESPONSIBILITIES WHEN PROVIDING INVESTMENT ADVICE

When securities professionals act in an investment advisory capacity, they act as fiduciaries and are held to higher ethical standards than when they are engaged in the sales of securities. Fiduciary responsibility exceeds that which is normally required of ordinary business relationships because the fiduciary is in a position of trust. A fiduciary must act for the benefit of the client and place the interests of clients above their own. When securities professionals provide advice for a fee, they have a higher level of responsibility as fiduciaries.

An IA or an IAR may be placed in the specific fiduciary position of trustee of a corporate retirement plan. Not only must they act solely for the benefit of the plan participants (the employees and the employer), but they must be careful to avoid engaging in any prohibited transactions. One of the most common examples used on the exam is when a C-level officer of the company (CEO, CFO, and so forth) approaches the trustee (IA or IAR) and suggests that the "plan" lend money to the company to help out with a short-term cash deficiency. That is not acceptable.

4. 4. 1   PRINCIPAL OR AGENCY TRANSACTIONS

The act prohibits an investment adviser from effecting transactions as a principal with his clients or as an agent for his clients, unless his clients receive full written disclosure as to the capacity in which the adviser proposes to act and consent to do so before the completion (settlement) of the proposed transaction. This is unlike a broker/dealer who, when acting as a principal in a trade with a customer or as the customer's agent, need only indicate that capacity on the trade confirmation; consent is not required.

The securities laws do not prohibit a registered investment adviser representative from being an employee of a registered broker/dealer. However, there would be a duty on the part of both the broker/dealer and the soliciting advisers to inform advisory clients of their ability to seek execution of transactions with broker/dealers other than those who have employed the advisers.

4. 4. 1. 1   Time of Consent

As stated, the Uniform Securities Act prohibits any adviser from engaging in or effecting a principal or agency transaction with a client without disclosing in writing to the client, "before the completion of such transaction," the capacity in which the adviser is acting and obtaining the client's consent to the transaction. It has been determined that a securities transaction is completed upon settlement, not upon execution. Implicit in the phrase "before the completion of such transaction" is the recognition that a securities transaction involves various stages before it is "complete." The phrase "completion of such transaction" on its face would appear to be the point at which all aspects of a securities transaction have come to an end. That ending point of a transaction is when the actual exchange of securities and payment occurs, which is known as *settlement*. The date of execution (i.e., the trade date) marks an earlier point of a securities transaction at which the parties have agreed to its terms and are contractually obligated to settle the transaction. Thus, an adviser may comply with the rules either by obtaining client consent prior to execution of a principal or agency transaction, or after execution but prior to settlement of the transaction.

When soliciting a client's post-execution, pre-settlement consent to a principal or agency transaction, an adviser should be able to provide the client with sufficient information regarding the transaction, including information regarding pricing, best price, and final commission charges, to enable the client to make an informed decision to consent to the transaction. The regulators agree that, if after execution but before settlement of the transaction, an adviser also provides a client with information that is sufficient to inform the client of the conflicts of interest faced by the adviser in engaging in the transaction, then the adviser will have provided the information necessary for the client to make an informed decision for purposes of the rule.

This consent is required for each transaction of this type. In a 1945 decision, federal law determined that "blanket" approval is not permitted.

QUICK QUIZ 4.B

1. The BJS Advisory Service maintains no custody of customer funds or securities, requires no substantial prepayments of fees, and does not have investment discretion over clients' accounts. Which of the following would have to be promptly disclosed to clients?

   I. The SEC has entered an order barring the executive vice president of the firm from association with any firm in the investment business.
   II. BJS has just been fined $3,500 by the NYSE.
   III. A civil suit has just been filed against BJS by one of its clients alleging that BJS made unsuitable recommendations.

   A. I and II
   B. I and III
   C. II and III
   D. None of the above

4. 4. 2 AGENCY CROSS TRANSACTIONS

In an **agency cross transaction**, the adviser (or IAR acting on behalf of the firm) acts as agent for both its advisory client and the party on the other side of the trade. Both acts will permit an adviser to engage in these transactions provided the adviser obtains prior written consent for these types of transactions from the client that discloses the following.

■ The adviser will be receiving commissions from both sides of the trade.

■ There is a potential conflict of interest because of the division of loyalties to both sides.

■ On at least an annual basis, the adviser furnishes a statement or summary of the account identifying the total number of such transactions and the total amount of all remuneration from these transactions.

■ The disclosure document conspicuously indicates that this arrangement may be terminated at any time.

■ No transaction is effected in which the same investment adviser or an investment adviser and any person controlling, controlled by, or under common control with that investment adviser recommended the transaction to both any seller and any purchaser.

These requirements do not relieve advisers of their duties to obtain best execution and best price for any transaction.

In addition to the prior consent, at or before the completion of each agency cross transaction, the client must be sent a written trade confirmation which includes:

- a statement of the nature of the transaction;

- the date, and if requested, the time of the transaction; and

- the source and amount of any remuneration to be received by the IA (or IAR) in connection with the transaction.

EXAMPLE   An adviser has a client who is conservative and another who generally looks for more aggressive positions. The conservative client calls and expresses concerns about the volatility of First Tech Internet Services, Inc., stating that he thinks this may be the best time to exit his position. The adviser agrees and mentions that he has a risk-taking client for whom First Tech is suitable and he'd like to "cross" the security between the two clients, charging a small commission to each of them. With the permission of both parties, this is not a violation.

TEST TOPIC ALERT   In an agency cross transaction, the adviser may not recommend the transaction to both parties of the trade.

4. 4. 3   UNIFORM PRUDENT INVESTORS ACT OF 1994 (UPIA)

Beginning with the dynamic growth of the stock markets in the late 1960s, the investment practices of fiduciaries experienced significant change. As a result, the Uniform Prudent Investor Act (UPIA) was passed in 1994 as an attempt to update trust investment laws in recognition of those many changes. The basic standards for anyone, not just an investment adviser, who has a fiduciary role are found in this act, which has been adopted by almost all states. Under the UPIA, fiduciaries are required to use skill and caution when making investment decisions with other people's money. The UPIA makes five fundamental alterations in the former criteria for prudent investing. Those changes are as follows.

- The standard of prudence is applied to any investment as part of the total portfolio, rather than to individual investments. In this context, the term *portfolio* means all of the trust's or estate's assets.

- The trade-off in all investments between risk and return is identified as the fiduciary's primary consideration.

- All categorical restrictions on types of investments have been removed; the trustee can invest in anything that plays an appropriate role in achieving the risk/return objectives of the trust and that meets the other requirements of prudent investing.

- The well-accepted requirement that fiduciaries diversify their investments has been integrated into the definition of prudent investing.

- The much-criticized former rule forbidding the trustee to delegate investment functions has been reversed. Delegation is now permitted, subject to safeguards.

With greater numbers of trustees delegating investment decisions to investment advisers, NASAA has determined that you must know how the UPIA affects their role. Here are some thoughts that will help you on the exam.

■ A trustee must invest and manage trust assets as a prudent investor would, by considering the purposes, terms, distribution requirements, and other circumstances of the trust. In satisfying this standard, the trustee must exercise reasonable care, skill, and caution.

■ A trustee's investment and management decisions about individual assets must be evaluated, not in isolation but in the context of the total portfolio and as a part of an overall investment strategy with risk and return objectives that are reasonably suited to the trust.

4. 5 GENERAL RULES APPLYING TO INVESTMENT ADVISERS

4. 5. 1 INVESTMENT ADVISORY CONTRACTS

The primary relationship between a client and an investment adviser is determined by an investment advisory contract. The USA makes it unlawful for an investment adviser to enter into, extend, or renew any investment advisory contract unless in writing, or the Administrator, by rule or order, provides otherwise.

Under the USA, an investment advisory contract must disclose:

■ the services to be provided including custody, if appropriate;

■ the term of the contract;

■ the amount of the advisory fee or the formula for computing the fee;

■ the amount or manner of calculation of the amount of any prepaid fee to be returned in the event of contract termination;

■ whether the contract grants discretionary power to the adviser or its representatives;

■ that no assignment of the contract may be made by the adviser without the consent of the other party to the contract; and

■ that, if the adviser is organized as a partnership, any change to a minority interest in the firm will be communicated to advisory clients within a reasonable period. A change to a majority of the partnership interests would be considered an assignment.

The act also prohibits certain performance fee arrangements contingent on capital gains or appreciation in the client's account. There is an exception, however, from the performance fee provisions for contracts with:

■ a registered investment company; or

■ any person with $750,000 under the adviser's management or a net worth of at least $1.5 million.

A fee based on the average amount of money under management over a particular period is not considered to be a performance fee.

TAKE NOTE

It is necessary for you to understand the technical definition of *assignment* as used in the acts. **Assignment** includes any direct or indirect transfer or pledge of an investment advisory contract by the adviser or of a controlling block of the adviser's outstanding voting securities by a stockholder of the adviser. If the investment adviser is a partnership, no assignment of an investment advisory contract is considered to result from the death or withdrawal of a minority of the partners or from the admission to the adviser of one or more partners who, after admission, will be only a minority interest in the business, whereas a change to a majority would be considered an assignment. However, a reorganization or similar activity that does not result in a change of actual control or management of an investment adviser is not an assignment.

TEST TOPIC ALERT

There are two additional points related to performance-based compensation that you must know. First, the adviser must use net performance—that is, consider both gains and losses. Second, as with so many other rules, the Administrator has the power to authorize this type of fee even when the stated conditions are not met.

CASE STUDY

Assignment and Notification of Change in Membership

Situation: Mr. Bixby withdrew $10 million from his account at the end of the year, leaving less than $750,000 under management with Market Tech Advisers, Inc., an advisory company incorporated in Illinois. During the course of the year, three officers left the firm. As a matter of corporate policy, Market Tech did not advise Mr. Bixby of these changes.

The following year, Market Tech (without notifying Mr. Bixby) assigned his account to Associated Investment Partners, a small partnership located in California, and Mr. Bixby was happy with the new partnership. Shortly after the assignment, Mr. Bixby learned of the death of one of the major partners through an article in the newspaper. He retained his account at Associated even though he had not been informed by them of the partner's death.

Analysis: Market Tech Advisers, Inc., was under no obligation to inform Mr. Bixby of the change in officers because it is a corporation and not a partnership. However, they did violate the USA by assigning Mr. Bixby's account to Associated Partners without his consent. Additionally, the USA requires partnerships to inform clients of any change in partner membership within a reasonable amount of time after the change, which means that Associated Partners violated the USA by not informing Mr. Bixby of the partner's death.

CASE STUDY

Investment Advisory Fees

Situation: Using the same client information as above, Market Tech Advisers, a registered investment advisory company, charges clients a fee of 1% of their assets managed by the firm on the basis of the average amount of funds in the account each quarter. In addition, for some of its high-net-worth clients, Market Tech charges a fee on the basis of the degree to which its performance exceeds that of the S&P 500. Last quarter, Market Tech's performance was extremely good and, as a result, the fees of one of its largest clients, Mr. Bixby, more than doubled. Next quarter, the value of the account dropped by 25% and so did the fee. Mr. Bixby complained that Market Tech was sharing in his capital appreciation in violation of the USA because he no longer had the required funds on deposit in the account.

Analysis: Market Tech is in compliance with the USA. Market Tech charged Mr. Bixby a 1% fee on the basis of the total assets in the account over a designated period as well as the stated performance fee. Because the assets increased and the performance beat the benchmark, so did the fee. Market Tech based its fees on the average value of funds under management and on a percentage of Mr. Bixby's capital gains—a practice in compliance with the USA for investors with a net worth at his level. Even though he no longer had $750,000 at the firm, his net worth was still in excess of $1.5 million. In the subsequent quarter, Market Tech's fee declined by 25% as a result of market deterioration. More than likely, no incentive fee was earned in this quarter.

TAKE NOTE

Any material legal action against the adviser must be disclosed to existing clients promptly. If the action occurred within the past 10 years, it must be disclosed to prospective clients not less than 48 hours before entering into the contract, or no later than the time of entering into such contract if the client has the right to terminate the contract without penalty within five business days.

Additionally, certain investment advisers are required to disclose any adverse financial condition that could impair the ability of the firm to perform its duties.

QUICK QUIZ 4.C

1. An investment advisory contract need not include
   A. the fees and their method of computation
   B. a statement prohibiting assignment of client accounts without client consent
   C. the states in which the adviser is licensed to conduct business
   D. notification requirement upon change in membership, if an investment partnership

   True or False?

   ____ 2. An Administrator may not prevent custody of securities or funds if an adviser notifies the Administrator before taking custody.

   ____ 3. An adviser may not sell securities to its customers from its own proprietary account.

   ____ 4. Under USA antifraud provisions, an investment adviser is bound by the restrictions that apply to sales practices when engaged in sales activities.

4. 5. 2 BROCHURE RULE

To provide some assurance that the act will not be violated, the regulators have recommended that each of the adviser's advisory clients be given a written statement (brochure) prepared by the adviser that makes all appropriate disclosures. The disclosure statement should include the nature and extent of any adverse interest of the adviser, including the amount of compensation he would receive in connection with the account. This is particularly important if the adviser will be receiving compensation from sources other than the agreed-upon advisory fee or that recommendations are limited to the firm's proprietary products. Furthermore, the adviser should, but is not required to, obtain a written acknowledgment from each of his clients of their receipt of the disclosure statement.

Because the brochure is really the only way the potential or existing client can learn about the investment adviser, disclosure must be made to all current clients and to prospective clients regarding material disciplinary action. The broadest definition of **material** would include any actions taken against the firm or management persons by a court or regulatory authority within the past 10 years. Required disclosure would include the following:

- State or regulatory proceedings in which the adviser or a management person was found to have violated rules or statutes that led to the denial, suspension, or revocation of the firm's or the individual management person's registration

- Court proceedings, such as a permanent or temporary injunction, against the firm or management person pertaining to an investment-related activity or any felony

- Self-regulatory organization proceedings in which the adviser or management person caused the business to lose its registration; the firm or individual was barred, suspended, or expelled; or a fine in excess of $2,500 or a limitation was placed on the adviser or management person's activities

You may remember that back in Unit 1, we mentioned that investment advisers registered with the Administrator use the Form ADV Parts 1 and 2. Unless otherwise provided in this rule, an investment adviser, registered or required to be registered under the Uniform Securities Act, must furnish each advisory client and prospective advisory client with:

- a brochure which may be a copy of Part 2A of its Form ADV or written documents containing the information required by Part 2A of Form ADV;

- a copy of its Part 2B brochure supplement for each individual who

  — provides investment advice and has direct contact with clients in this state, or

  — exercises discretion over assets of clients in this state, even if no direct contact is involved;

- a copy of its Part 2A Appendix 1 wrap fee brochure if the investment adviser sponsors or participates in a wrap fee account;

- a summary of material changes, which may be included in Form ADV Part 2 or given as a separate document; and

- such other information as the Administrator may require.

4. 5. 2. 1   Brochure Delivery Requirements

The NASAA Model Rule dealing with investment adviser brochures has very specific delivery requirements, both at the initial phase of contact and on an ongoing basis.

4. 5. 2. 1. 1   Initial Delivery

An investment adviser, except as discussed below, must deliver the Part 2A brochure and any Part 2B brochure supplements required by the rule to a prospective advisory client:

- not less than 48 hours prior to entering into any advisory contract with such client or prospective client; or
- at the time of entering into any such contract, if the advisory client has a right to terminate the contract without penalty within five business days after entering into the contract.

4. 5. 2. 1. 2   Annual Delivery

An investment adviser, except discussed below, must:

- deliver within 120 days of the end of its fiscal year a free, updated brochure and related brochure supplements which include or are accompanied by a summary of material changes; or
- deliver a summary of material changes that includes an offer to provide a copy of the updated brochure and supplements and information on how the client may obtain a copy of the brochures and supplements.

TAKE NOTE   Investment advisers do not have to deliver a summary of material changes or a brochure to clients if no material changes have taken place since the last summary and brochure delivery.

---

4. 5. 2. 1. 3   Exceptions to the Brochure Delivery Requirements

Delivery of the brochure and related brochure supplements need not be made to:

- clients who receive only impersonal advice and who pay less than $500 in fees per year; or
- an investment company registered under the Investment Company Act of 1940.

TEST TOPIC ALERT   For the purpose of the brochure rule, "contract for impersonal advisory services" means any contract relating solely to the provision of investment advisory services:

- by means of written material or oral statements which do not purport to meet the objectives or needs of specific individuals or accounts;
- through the issuance of statistical information containing no expression of opinion as to the investment merits of a particular security; or
- any combination of the above services.

---

4. 5. 2. 1. 4   Electronic Delivery of the Brochure

Delivery of the brochure and related supplements may be made electronically if the investment adviser:

- in the case of an initial delivery to a potential client, obtains a verification that a readable copy of the brochure and supplements were received by the client;
- in cases other than initial deliveries, obtains each client's prior consent to provide the brochure and supplements electronically;
- prepares the electronically delivered brochure and supplements in the format prescribed in the instructions to Form ADV Part 2;

■ delivers the brochure and supplements in a format that can be retained by the client in either electronic or paper form; and

■ establishes procedures to supervise personnel transmitting the brochure and supplements and prevent violations of this rule.

4. 5. 2. 2 Wrap Fee Programs

The rules on disclosure are somewhat different for wrap fee programs. A **wrap fee program** is a program under which a client is charged a specified fee, or fees, not based directly on transactions in a client's account, for investment advisory services (which may include portfolio management or advice concerning the selection of other investment advisers) and for execution of client transactions.

Any registered investment adviser compensated under a wrap fee program for sponsoring, organizing, or administering the program, or for selecting, or providing advice to clients regarding the selection of, other investment advisers in the program, does not use the normal brochure (Part 2A of the ADV). Instead, that adviser furnishes clients and prospective clients a document known as the Form ADV Part 2A, Appendix 1 which details the nature and expenses involved with the wrap fee program(s).

One final point to remember about wrap fee programs is that it is essential for the IA (or IAR) to explain to prospects that buying *a la carte* (the services individually) might be less expensive than the wrap program. This is especially true for the investor who does limited trading, like those who follow the *buy and hold* strategy.

4. 5. 2. 3 Updating the Form ADV

The Form ADV must be updated each year by filing an annual updating amendment within 90 days after the end of the adviser's fiscal year. This annual updating amendment is used to update the responses to all items on the ADV. Of critical importance is the verification of assets under management (AUM) ensuring that the adviser is eligible to continue being registered with the state(s) or may have to move to SEC registration. One of the requirements relating to the brochure described in Part 2A of the Form ADV is that submission must be made of a summary of material changes either in the brochure (cover page or the page immediately thereafter) or as an exhibit to the brochure.

4. 5. 2. 3. 1 Amendments for Material Changes

In addition to the annual updating amendment, the IA must amend the Form ADV by filing additional amendments promptly if information relating to any of the following changes or becomes inaccurate in any way:

■ Change of the registrant's name

■ Change in the principal business location

■ Change in the location of books and records, if they are kept somewhere other than at the principal location

■ Change to the contact person preparing the form

■ Change in organizational structure, such as from partnership to corporation and so on

■ Information provided in the brochure becomes materially inaccurate

■ Change to any of the questions regarding disciplinary actions

■ Change in policy regarding custody of the customer funds and/or securities

4. 5. 3   CUSTODY OF CLIENT FUNDS AND SECURITIES

Under the USA, it is unlawful for an adviser to have custody of client funds and securities if:

- the Administrator in the state prohibits, by rule, advisers from having custody;
- in absence of a rule, an adviser fails to notify the Administrator that he has custody;
- the adviser fails to supply clients, no less frequently than quarterly, with a statement of account activity and the location and amount of their assets;
- the adviser does not use a qualified custodian who maintains those funds and securities

    — in a separate account for each client under that client's name, or

    — in accounts that contain only the investment adviser's clients' funds and securities, under the investment adviser's name as agent or trustee for the clients, or, in the case of a pooled investment vehicle that the investment adviser manages, in the name of the pooled investment vehicle; and

- the client funds and securities of which the investment adviser has custody are not verified by actual examination at least once during each calendar year. The audit must be done by an independent certified public accountant, pursuant to a written agreement between the investment adviser and the independent certified public accountant. This must be a surprise audit so it is at a time that is chosen by the independent certified public accountant without prior notice or announcement to the investment adviser and that is irregular from year to year.

TEST TOPIC ALERT   If an investment adviser wishes to maintain custody of customer funds or securities, and state law does not prohibit doing so, the adviser must give written notice to the Administrator. Do not choose the answer on the exam that states, "must obtain permission from the Administrator." All that is required is notification.

4. 5. 3. 1   Definition of Custody

Custody means holding directly or indirectly, client funds or securities, or having any authority to obtain possession of them. The investment adviser has custody if a related person (any person, directly or indirectly, controlling or controlled by the investment adviser; and any person that is under common control with the investment adviser) holds, directly or indirectly, client funds or securities, or has any authority to obtain possession of them, in connection with advisory services the investment adviser provides to clients.

Custody includes:

- possession of client funds or securities unless received inadvertently and returned to the sender promptly, but in any case within three business days of receiving them;
- any arrangement (including a general power of attorney) under which you are authorized or permitted to withdraw client funds or securities maintained with a custodian upon your instruction to the custodian; and
- any capacity (such as general partner of a limited partnership, managing member of a limited liability company or a comparable position for another type of pooled investment vehicle, or trustee of a trust) that gives you or your supervised person legal ownership of or access to client funds or securities.

Custody does *not* include:

- receipt of checks drawn by clients and made payable to unrelated third parties if forwarded to the third party within three days (72 hours) of receipt; and
- having investment discretion over the client's account.

Custody is the physical possession or control of funds and securities. Many advisers do not have custody because their client funds and securities are maintained at a bank or brokerage house. The adviser makes investment decisions under an advisory contract even though the client's funds and securities are placed in a custodial account at a commercial bank. Most Administrators will require advisers who maintain custody to provide a surety bond or meet certain net worth standards.

TAKE NOTE
A major benefit of having the qualified custodian do all of the work is that the investment adviser is relieved of the minimum net worth requirement of $35,000 and the obligation to furnish clients with an annual audited balance sheet. However, if the investment adviser exercises discretion, the $10,000 net worth requirement is still in effect.

4. 5. 3. 2 Exceptions to the Custody Rule

Shares of mutual funds are an exception to the custody rule. With respect to shares of an open-end company as defined in the Investment Company Act of 1940 (mutual fund), the investment adviser may use the mutual fund's transfer agent in lieu of a qualified custodian for purposes of complying with this rule.

Fee deduction is another exception to the custody rule. An investment adviser is not required to obtain an independent verification of client funds and securities maintained by a qualified custodian if all of the following are met:

- The investment adviser has custody of the funds and securities solely as a consequence of its authority to make withdrawals from client accounts to pay its advisory fee
- The investment adviser has written authorization from the client to deduct advisory fees from the account held with the qualified custodian
- Each time a fee is directly deducted from a client account, the investment adviser concurrently:

  — sends the qualified custodian an invoice or statement of the amount of the fee to be deducted from the client's account, and

  — sends the client an invoice or statement itemizing the fee. Itemization includes the formula used to calculate the fee, the amount of assets under management the fee is based on, and the time period covered by the fee.

- The investment adviser notifies the Administrator in writing that the investment adviser intends to use the safeguards provided above.

4. 5. 4 PERIODIC INSPECTIONS OF INVESTMENT ADVISERS

During routine inspections, the Administrator, or his designee, reviews an investment adviser's filings with the SEC (if federal covered) or Administrator and other materials provided to clients to ensure that the adviser's disclosures are accurate and timely and do not omit material information. Examples of failures to disclose material information to clients would include the following.

- An adviser fails to disclose all fees that a client would pay in connection with the advisory contract, including how fees are charged and whether fees are negotiable.

- An adviser fails to disclose his affiliation with a broker/dealer or other securities professionals or issuers.

- If an adviser has discretionary authority or custody over a client's funds or securities, or requires prepayment of advisory fees of more than $500 from a client, six or more months in advance (sometimes referred to as a *substantial prepayment* on the exam), the adviser fails to disclose a financial condition that is reasonably likely to impair the ability of the adviser to meet contractual commitments to those clients.

TAKE NOTE   Although the Administrator's jurisdiction is somewhat limited when it comes to federal covered advisers, since those advisers are liable under the USA's anti-fraud provisions, he is authorized to conduct these inspections.

4. 6 SECTION 28(e) SAFE HARBOR

Research is the foundation of the money management industry. Providing research is one important, long-standing service of the brokerage business. Soft-dollar arrangements have developed as a link between the brokerage industry's supply of research and the money management industry's demand for research. What does that mean and how does it work? To find the answers, we must review the provisions of Section 28(e) of the Securities Exchange Act of 1934.

Broker/dealers typically provide a bundle of services, including research and execution of transactions. The research provided can be either proprietary (created and provided by the broker/dealer, including tangible research products as well as access to analysts and traders) or third party (created by a third party but provided by the broker/dealer). Because commission dollars pay for the entire bundle of services, the practice of allocating certain of these dollars to pay for the research component has come to be called *soft dollars*. The SEC has defined soft-dollar practices as arrangements under which products or services other than execution of securities transactions are obtained by an adviser from or through a broker/dealer in exchange for the direction by the adviser of client brokerage transactions to the broker/dealer, frequently referred to as *directed transactions* on the exam. Under traditional fiduciary principles, a fiduciary cannot use assets entrusted by clients to benefit itself. As the SEC has recognized, when an adviser uses client commissions to buy research from a broker/dealer, it receives a benefit because it is relieved from the need to produce or pay for the research itself. In addition, when transactions involving soft dollars involve the adviser paying up or receiving executions at inferior prices, advisers using soft dollars face a conflict of interest between their need to obtain research and their clients' interest in paying the lowest commission rate available and obtaining the best possible execution.

Soon after May 1, 1975 (May Day), when the SEC abolished fixed commission rates, Congress created a safe harbor under Section 28(e) of the Securities Exchange Act of 1934 to protect advisers from claims that they had breached their fiduciary duties by causing clients to pay more than the lowest available commission rates in exchange for research and execution.

Because of the conflict of interest that exists when an investment adviser receives research, products, or other services as a result of allocating brokerage on behalf of clients, the SEC requires advisers to disclose soft-dollar arrangements to their clients. Section 28(e) provides that a person who exercises investment discretion with respect to an account will not be deemed to have acted unlawfully or to have breached a fiduciary duty solely by reason of his having caused the account to pay more than the lowest available commission if such person determines in good faith that the amount of the commission is reasonable in relation to the value of the brokerage and research services provided.

In adopting Section 28(e), Congress acknowledged the important service broker/dealers provide by producing and distributing investment research to money managers. Section 28(e) defines when a person is deemed to be providing brokerage and research services, and states that a person provides brokerage and research services insofar as he:

■ furnishes advice directly or through publications or writing about the value of securities, the advisability of investing in, purchasing, or selling securities, or the availability of purchasers or sellers of securities;

■ furnishes analyses and reports concerning issuers, industries, securities, economic factors and trends, portfolio strategy, and performance of accounts; or

■ effects securities transactions and performs functions incidental thereto (such as clearance, settlement, and custody).

Finally, Section 28(e)(2) grants the SEC rulemaking authority to require that investment advisers disclose their soft-dollar policies and procedures.

An adviser is obligated under both the Investment Advisers Act of 1940 and state law to act in the best interests of its client. This duty generally precludes the adviser from using client assets for its own benefit or the benefit of other clients, without obtaining the client's consent based on full and fair disclosure. In such a situation, the antifraud provisions of the federal securities laws also would require full and fair disclosure to the client of all material facts concerning the arrangement. As the SEC has stated, "the adviser may not use its client's assets for its own benefit without prior consent, even if it costs the client nothing extra." Consent may be expressly provided by the client; consent also may be inferred from all of the facts and circumstances, including the adviser's disclosure in its Form ADV.

It also should be noted that Section 28(e) only excuses paying more than the lowest available commission. It does not shield a person who exercises investment discretion from charges of violations of the antifraud provisions of the federal securities laws arising from churning an account, failing to obtain the best price or best execution, or failing to make required disclosure.

Section 28(e) does not relieve investment advisers of their disclosure obligations under the federal securities laws. Disclosure is required whether the product or service acquired by the adviser using soft dollars is inside or outside of the safe harbor. Advisers are required to disclose, among other things, the products and services received through soft-dollar arrangements, regardless of whether the safe harbor applies.

Registered investment advisers must disclose to clients certain information about their brokerage allocation policies in Part 2A of Form ADV. Specifically, if the value of products, research, and services provided to an investment adviser is a factor in selecting brokers to execute client trades, the investment adviser must describe in its Form ADV:

■ the products, research, and services;

■ whether clients may pay commissions higher than those obtainable from other brokers in return for the research, products, and services;

■ whether research is used to service all accounts or just those accounts paying for it; and

■ any procedures that the adviser used during the last fiscal year to direct client transactions to a particular broker in return for products, research and services received.

The purpose of this disclosure is to provide clients with material information about the adviser's brokerage selection practices that may be important to clients in deciding to hire or continue a contract with an adviser and that will permit them to evaluate any conflicts of interest inherent in the adviser's policies and practices. In this respect, the SEC and courts have stated that disclosure is required, even when there is only a potential conflict of interest.

It is important to note, however, that disclosure in the Form ADV may not satisfy an adviser's full obligation to disclose soft-dollar arrangements. For example, Part 2A of Form ADV, or the adviser's brochure, must be delivered only at the commencement of the advisory relationship, and delivered only annually thereafter. Thus, an adviser may have to update Part 2A and provide existing clients with additional disclosure whenever material changes occur in its soft-dollar practices.

TEST TOPIC ALERT

What this all comes down to is knowing what is and what is not included in the safe harbor. Here are some of the items that, if received as soft-dollar compensation, would likely fall under 28(e)'s safe harbor:

- Research reports analyzing the performance of a particular company or stock
- Financial newsletters and trade journals could be eligible research if they relate with appropriate specificity
- Quantitative analytical software
- Seminars or conferences with appropriate content
- Effecting and clearing securities trades

The following would be likely to fall out of the safe harbor:

- Telephone lines
- Office furniture, including computer hardware
- Travel expenses associated with attending seminars
- Rent
- Any software that does not relate directly to analysis of securities
- Payment for training courses for this exam
- Internet service

QUICK QUIZ 4.D

1. Which of the following would NOT be included in the safe harbor provisions of Section 28(e) of the Securities Exchange Act of 1934?

   A. Proprietary research
   B. Third-party research
   C. Rent
   D. Seminar registration fees

2. When an investment adviser with discretion over a client's account directs trade executions to a specific broker/dealer and uses the commission dollars generated to acquire software that analyzes technical market trends, it is known as

   A. hard-dollar compensation
   B. indirect compensation
   C. investment discretion
   D. soft-dollar compensation

4. 7 USING THE INTERNET

Obviously, there was no Internet when the Uniform Securities Act was written in 1956. As with other changes in the way we do business, NASAA has written Model Rules to update the regulatory scheme. One example is broker/dealers and investment advisers using the Internet. A firm's website, considered advertising, can be seen everywhere. Does that mean the firm has a place of business in the state? Without getting too technical, there are several requirements to insure that the person is not deemed to be in the state.

- The communication clearly states that the person may only do business in this state if properly registered or exempt from registration.

- Any follow-up individualized responses with prospects in this state that involve either the effecting or attempting to effect transactions in securities, or the rendering of personalized investment advice for compensation, as may be, will not be made without compliance with state broker/dealer, investment adviser, agent, or IA representative registration requirements, or an applicable exemption or exclusion.

- The site may only make available general information, no specific advice or recommendations.

- In the case of an agent or IAR

  — the affiliation with the broker/dealer or investment adviser of the agent or IAR is prominently disclosed within the communication;

  — the broker/dealer or investment adviser with whom the agent or IAR is associated retains responsibility for reviewing and approving the content of any Internet communication by an agent or IAR;

  — the broker/dealer or investment adviser with whom the agent or IAR is associated first authorizes the distribution of information on the particular products and services through the Internet communication; and

  — in disseminating information through the Internet communication, the agent or IAR rep acts within the scope of the authority granted by the broker/dealer or investment adviser.

What this basically means is that if you just generally advertise on the Internet, you don't have to be registered in the state. BUT, if you follow-up with advice (IAR) or offering securities (agent), you either have to register or find some kind of exemption.

TEST TOPIC ALERT   Broker/dealers, but *not* investment advisers, are permitted to use testimonials in advertisements. Therefore, a broker/dealer's Website could contain praise from clients as well as details of the firm's community involvement. However, nothing could ever be used that might be construed as an endorsement or approval from the Administrator.

4. 8 SALES OF SECURITIES AT FINANCIAL INSTITUTIONS

The 1990s saw a proliferation of broker/dealer services being offered on the premises of financial institutions, particularly banks. In response to the potential for confusion as well as conflicts of interest, NASAA prepared Model Rules for sales of securities at financial institutions which were adopted October 6, 1998. Here are the key points for you to know.

No broker/dealer shall conduct broker/dealer services on the premises of a financial institution where retail deposits (that means from ordinary customers like you and me) are taken unless the broker/dealer complies initially and continuously with the following requirements.

4. 8. 1 SETTING

Wherever practical, broker/dealer services shall be conducted in a physical location distinct from the area in which the financial institution's retail deposits are taken. In those situations where there is insufficient space to allow separate areas, the broker/dealer has a heightened responsibility to distinguish its services from those of the financial institution. The broker/dealer's name shall be clearly displayed in the area in which the broker/dealer conducts its services.

4. 8. 2 CUSTOMER DISCLOSURE AND WRITTEN ACKNOWLEDGMENT

At or prior to the time that a customer's securities brokerage account is opened by a broker/dealer on the premises of a financial institution where retail deposits are taken, the broker/dealer must:

- disclose, **orally** and **in writing**, that the securities products purchased or sold in a transaction with the broker/dealer

  — are not insured by the Federal Deposit Insurance Corporation (FDIC),

  — are not deposits or other obligations of the financial institution and are not guaranteed by the financial institution, and

  — are subject to investment risks, including possible loss of the principal invested; and

- make reasonable efforts to obtain from each customer, during the account opening process, a written acknowledgment of the disclosures.

4. 8. 3 COMMUNICATIONS WITH THE PUBLIC

The following logo format disclosures may be used by a broker/dealer in advertisements and sales literature, including material published, or designed for use, in radio or television broadcasts, Automated Teller Machine (ATM) screens, billboards, signs, posters, and brochures, to comply with the requirements, provided that such disclosures are displayed in a conspicuous manner:

- Not FDIC Insured
- No Bank Guarantee
- May Lose Value

As long as the omission of the disclosures would not cause the advertisement or sales literature to be misleading in light of the context in which the material is presented, such disclosures are not required with respect to messages contained in:

- radio broadcasts of **30 seconds** or less;
- electronic signs, including billboard-type signs that are electronic, time, and temperature signs and ticker tape signs, but excluding messages contained in such media as television, on-line computer services, or ATMs; and
- signs, such as banners and posters, when used only as location indicators.

4. 8. 4   SIPC COVERAGE

While most people are familiar with FDIC insurance and the role it plays insuring client accounts at banks, insurance from the Securities Investors Protection Corporation (SIPC) is less well known. SIPC provides protection to clients of broker/dealers in the event the B/D enters bankruptcy proceedings. SIPC (not the Administrator) appoints a trustee whose job it is to return assets owned by clients, but held at the B/D. SIPC does *not* protect against a decline in the value of the client's portfolio. As with FDIC, there are limits to the coverage, but those will not be tested.

4. 9 CURRENCY TRANSACTION REPORTS (CTRS)

The Bank Secrecy Act requires every financial institution to file a Currency Transaction Report (CTR) on FinCEN Form 104 for each cash transaction that exceeds $10,000. This requirement applies to cash transactions used to pay off loans, the electronic transfer of funds, or the purchase of certificates of deposit, stock, bonds, mutual funds, or other investments.

UNIT TEST

1. Market manipulation is one of the prohibited practices under the Uniform Securities Act. Which of the following is an example of a broker/dealer engaging in market manipulation?

   I. Churning
   II. Arbitrage
   III. Wash trade
   IV. Matched orders

   A. I and II
   B. I, III and IV
   C. III and IV
   D. IV only

2. Your customer called to check on her account value at 9:00 am. You were unavailable at the time. It is now 2:00 pm, and you are able to call her back. Between 9:00 am and 2:00 pm, her account value dropped from $11,500 to $10,000. What should you say to her?

   A. "At the time you called, your account had a value of $10,000."
   B. "Your account value cannot be determined until the market closes."
   C. "Your account is valued at $10,000 at this time."
   D. "Your account was down to $9,700 earlier today but is now up to $10,000."

3. All of the following are prohibited practices under the USA EXCEPT

   I. borrowing money or securities from the account of a former banker with express written permission
   II. failing to identify a customer's financial objectives
   III. selling unregistered non-exempt securities to a closed-end investment company
   IV. supplying funds to a client's account only when or if it declines below a preagreed-upon level

   A. I and II
   B. I, II and III
   C. II and IV
   D. III only

4. A customer is upset with her agent for not servicing her account properly and sends him a complaint letter about his actions. Under the Uniform Securities Act, the agent should

   A. call the customer, apologize, and attempt to correct the problem
   B. tell the customer he is willing to make rescission
   C. do nothing
   D. bring the customer complaint to his employer immediately

5. Under the USA, the Administrator may suspend or revoke a registration if an agent

   I. borrows money from his wealthy clients' accounts
   II. solicits retail orders for nonexempt unregistered securities
   III. buys and sells securities in accounts to generate a high level of commissions
   IV. alters market quotations to induce a client to invest in an attractive growth stock

   A. I, II and III
   B. I and III
   C. I and IV
   D. I, II, III and IV

6. Under the Uniform Securities Act, an investment adviser may legally have custody of money or securities belonging to a client if the

   I. adviser is not bonded
   II. Administrator has not prohibited custodial arrangements
   III. adviser does not also have discretionary authority over the account
   IV. adviser has notified the Administrator that he has custody

   A. I and III
   B. II only
   C. II and IV
   D. IV only

7. According to the USA, which of the following is an example of market manipulation?
   A. Creating the illusion of active trading
   B. Omitting material facts in a presentation
   C. Guaranteeing performance of a security
   D. Transacting in excess of a customer's financial capability

8. In 1998, NASAA promulgated a Model Rule covering the sales of securities at financial institutions. Under that rule, an advertisement by a broker/dealer would be exempt from meeting certain disclosure requirements of that rule if
   A. it was distributed to a limited demographic group
   B. the broker/dealer and the bank were affiliated
   C. it were a radio ad not exceeding 30 seconds as long as the omission of the required disclosures would not cause the advertisement to be misleading in light of the context in which the material is presented
   D. the advertisement only related to NYSE listed stocks

9. Which of the following practices is prohibited under the USA?
   A. Participating in active trading of a security in which an unusually high trading volume has occurred
   B. Offering services that an agent cannot realistically perform because of his broker/dealer's limitations
   C. Altering the customer's order at the request of a customer, which subsequently results in a substantial loss
   D. Failing to inform the firm's principal of frequent oral customer complaints

10. An agent hears a rumor concerning a security and uses the rumor to convince a client to purchase the security. Under the USA, the agent may
    A. recommend the security if it is an appropriate investment
    B. recommend the investment if the rumor is based on material inside information
    C. recommend the security if the source of the rumor is reliable
    D. not recommend the security

11. If an agent thought that a technology stock was undervalued and actively solicited 75% of his customers to buy the stock, the agent
    I. did not violate the USA if all material facts were disclosed
    II. committed an unethical sales practice because the firm has not recommended this technology stock
    III. committed an unethical business practice
    IV. did not commit a violation if all clients were accurately informed of the price of the stock
    A. I, II and IV
    B. I and IV
    C. III only
    D. I, II, III and IV

12. Which of the following transactions are prohibited?
    I. Borrowing money or securities from a high net worth customer
    II. Selling speculative issues to a retired couple of modest means on a fixed income
    III. Failing to follow a customer's orders so as to prevent investment in a security not adequately covered by well-known securities analysts
    IV. Backdating confirmations for the benefit of the client's tax reporting
    A. I and II
    B. I, II and III
    C. II and III
    D. I, II, III and IV

13. It is legal under the USA for an agent to tell a client that
    A. a registered security may lawfully be sold in that state
    B. an exempt security is not required to be registered because it is generally regarded as being safer than a nonexempt security
    C. the agent's qualifications have been found satisfactory by the Administrator
    D. a registered security has been approved for sale in the state by the Administrator

14. An agent omits facts that a prudent investor requires to make informed decisions. Under the Uniform Securities Act, this action is
    A. fraudulent for nonexempt securities only
    B. fraudulent for exempt securities only
    C. fraudulent for both exempt and nonexempt securities
    D. not fraudulent if there was willful intent to omit the information

15. Which of the following actions is NOT a prohibited practice under the USA?
    A. An agent places an order to purchase a stock ahead of a large institutional order he has just received for that stock.
    B. An agent receives an unsolicited order from a client to purchase 200 shares of XYZ ten seconds after he has turned in his own order for that stock. It turns out that the agent acquired the shares for less than the client and does not make up the difference.
    C. A principal of a broker/dealer allows a rumor to spread that ABC is going to acquire LMN; after a few days, the broker/dealer sells ABC short for its own account.
    D. An agent sells a customer's stock at the bid price and makes up the difference with a personal check.

16. Which of the following is(are) prohibited under the USA?
    I. Recommending tax shelters to low-income retirees
    II. Stating that a state Administrator has approved an offering on the basis of the quality of information found in the prospectus
    III. Soliciting non-institutional orders for unregistered, nonexempt securities
    IV. Employing any device to defraud
    A. I only
    B. I and II
    C. I, II and III
    D. I, II, III and IV

17. According to the Uniform Securities Act, an investment adviser may have custody of a customer's funds and securities if
    A. it has received the permission of the Administrator
    B. it has received permission from the SEC
    C. it does not share in the capital gains of the account
    D. the Administrator has been informed of the custody

18. According to the USA, which of the following is a prohibited activity?
    A. The agent enters into an agreement to share in the profits/losses of the customer's account without the written consent of his broker/dealer.
    B. The agent and his spouse jointly own their own personal trading account at the firm.
    C. The agent, with his firm's and the client's written permission, participates in the profits and losses of the customer's account.
    D. An agent refuses a client's request to share in the performance of the client's account.

19. A registered broker/dealer is under common control with a registered investment adviser. An individual who is an agent of the broker/dealer and an investment adviser representative of the adviser has a client with $250,000 under an asset management program. This individual calls the client and suggests the purchase of 500 shares of RMBM common stock as an appropriate addition to the portfolio. The broker/dealer is a market maker in RMBM, and the sale will be made as a principal, a fact that is disclosed to the client on the trade confirmation. In this situation, the registered person has acted

    A. lawfully in that the disclosure of capacity was made on the confirmation
    B. lawfully in that disclosure of capacity is not necessary when executing trades in managed accounts
    C. unlawfully in that any stock in which the broker/dealer is a market maker is probably not suitable for a managed money client
    D. unlawfully in that investment advisers are required to make written disclosure before completion of a trade in which the firm or an affiliate will be acting in a principal capacity and receive the client's consent

20. Which of the following are prohibited practices?

    I. An investment advisory firm organized as a partnership failed to inform its clients of the departure of a partner with a very small interest in the partnership.
    II. An investment advisory firm charges an annual fee equal to 2% of the first $250,000 in assets under management, 1% of the next $500,000, and .5% for everything in excess of $750,000.
    III. The majority stockholder of a registered investment adviser pledges his stock as collateral for a loan taken out by the firm to expand its services without obtaining client consent for assignment of their contracts.
    IV. An adviser engages in agency cross transactions.

    A. I and III
    B. I and IV
    C. III and IV
    D. I, II, III and IV

21. ZAP Brokerage has 5 partners. Raymond Zap, Jr., is a minor partner. He violates the USA because he did not perform his job of making sure that the firm maintained the minimum required capital. Which of the following are TRUE?

    I. Only Raymond will have his license suspended.
    II. The Administrator may revoke the entire firm's right to sell securities.
    III. A revocation of ZAP's registration would cause each of its agent's registrations to be terminated.
    IV. The firm could be fined up to $5,000 but incur no suspension.

    A. I and II
    B. II and III
    C. III and IV
    D. I, II, III and IV

22. When may the intentional omission of a fact in a securities transaction constitute fraud?

    A. If a reasonable person would attach decision-making importance to the omitted information
    B. Only if the information was known beyond all doubt to be factual
    C. Only in the case of a new issue of securities
    D. Any time the information is known by fewer than 25 persons

23. Under the Uniform Securities Act, all of the following are prohibited practices EXCEPT

    A. making recommendations on the basis of material, nonpublic information
    B. making recommendations on the basis of material information after that information has been publicly released
    C. making recommendations without having reasonable grounds for believing they are suitable
    D. stating that recommendations have been approved by the Administrator

24. Under the Uniform Securities Act, all of the following are prohibited business practices EXCEPT

    A. failing to indicate that securities prices are subject to market fluctuation
    B. ignoring an order to buy a stock immediately at the market price because the price is falling and the customer will likely get a better price by waiting
    C. telling a customer that commission, taxes, and other costs will be higher than normal even when you do not know exactly how high they will be
    D. wash trades and matching orders to create the appearance of market activity

25. Which of the following activities of an investment advisory firm would not require consent of the clients of that advisory firm?

    A. The retirement of a sole proprietor investment adviser wishing to sell the practice to another investment adviser
    B. The chief operating officer of an investment advisory firm wishing to pledge her majority interest in the firm to a local bank for a loan to purchase an office building that will be leased to the advisory firm
    C. A minority partner resigning from the firm to start his own advisory firm
    D. An investment adviser wishing to merge with a larger, national advisory firm

26. Which of the following investment advisory contracts would be lawful?

    I. An investment advisory contract for ABC Mutual Fund providing that the investment adviser will be paid 1% of the fund's net asset value as of the last business day of June and December
    II. An investment advisory contract providing that the adviser will receive 5% of any increase in the client's capital assets as of the end of each calendar year
    III. An investment advisory contract specifying that the investment adviser will receive 2% of the first $10,000 of profit and 1% of all profit over $10,000 in the client's account at the end of each quarter
    IV. An investment advisory contract providing that the adviser is to receive ½% of the monthly value of the funds in the client's account averaged over a 12-month period

    A. I and II
    B. I and IV
    C. I, II, III and IV
    D. None of the above

27. Making recommendations on the basis of material inside information about an issuer or its securities, when this information has not been made public, is prohibited. Therefore, an agent or broker/dealer doing which of the following would be engaging in a fraudulent practice?

    I. Giving inside information to privileged clients without a fee
    II. Informing other issuers about the inside information with the intent of collectively taking advantage of the information
    III. Having your relatives in another state invest heavily in this security when it appears in the market
    IV. Investing large sums of the firm's money in this issue with the written consent of all partners

    A. I and III
    B. I and IV
    C. II and IV
    D. I, II, III and IV

28. You have a wealthy client who complains to you about the extremely low rates currently being offered by his bank on CDs. You tell him that you are willing to borrow up to $100,000 for 2 years at prime +1 and will deposit securities you own as collateral. Under the Uniform Securities Act
    A. it is prohibited to borrow money from a client unless the client is in the money lending business
    B. it is always prohibited to pay a client more than a bank CD rate
    C. it could be permitted if the proper disclosures were made
    D. approval of the appropriate supervisor of your firm would be required

29. A client has a cash account at his broker/dealer. Now, he wishes to open a margin account as well. Which of the following best describes the action that must be taken?
    A. Verbal instructions to open the account are sufficient because the customer relationship already exists.
    B. The customer must make the request in writing, either by mail or by fax.
    C. The firm must obtain a properly executed written margin agreement promptly after the initial transaction in the account.
    D. The customer must physically present himself at the agent's office and sign the appropriate papers.

30. Broker/dealer A wants to promote and reward teamwork. The firm plans to pay out a small percentage of year-end profits to the clerical staff as a bonus for their hard work. Under NASAA rules, is this permitted?
    A. Yes, if the bonuses are equally divided
    B. Yes, if all the agents agree to it
    C. Yes, if the clerical staff are all registered agents of the firm
    D. Yes, as long as the compensation is not sales related

ANSWERS AND RATIONALES

1. **C.** A wash trade, the practice of attempting to create the appearance of trading activity by entering offsetting buy and sell orders, is a form of market manipulation. Matched orders occur when market participants agree to buy and sell securities among themselves to create the appearance of heightened market activity; this is also a form of market manipulation. Although churning is a prohibited practice, it does not involve manipulating the market, and arbitrage is the perfectly legal practice of buying a security in one marketplace and simultaneously selling it in another to benefit from a price disparity.

2. **C.** All other choices are clearly a misrepresentation of account status.

3. **D.** It is permissible to sell unregistered non-exempt securities to an institutional buyer, such as an investment company, because that would be an exempt transaction. Borrowing money or securities from other than a bank or broker/dealer in the business of lending, failing to identify a customer's financial objectives, and guaranteeing a customer's account against losses are all prohibited practices.

4. **D.** Failure to bring customers' written complaints to the attention of the agent's broker/dealer is prohibited.

5. **D.** An Administrator may suspend or revoke an agent's registration if the agent engages in prohibited practices such as those described in each of the choices in the question. A retail order is one with a non-institutional client (think individual).

6. **C.** The Administrator may prohibit advisers from having custody of client funds or securities. If no such prohibition applies, the Administrator must be notified in writing if an adviser has custody. In almost all jurisdictions, a bond or sufficient net worth is required to maintain custody. Discretionary authority does not affect an adviser's ability to have custody.

7. **A.** Creating the illusion of trading activity is market manipulation. Guaranteeing performance of a security and omitting material facts are prohibited practices but do not constitute market manipulation. Trades too large for a customer are also prohibited because they are not suitable, but they are not market manipulation.

8. **C.** Under this Model rule, certain disclosures must be made. They include statements that even though the investments are being sold on the premises of a financial institution (typically a bank), they are not FDIC insured, may lose money, and are not an obligation of the bank. However, an exception from those required disclosures is made in the case of a short (no longer than 30 seconds) radio advertisement as long as there is nothing in that ad that could be construed as misleading without those disclaimers.

9. **B.** An agent may not offer services that he cannot perform. An agent may participate actively in trading a security in which an unusually high trading volume has occurred, provided the trading is not designed to create a false appearance of high volume. At the client's request, an agent can alter a client's order, even if the change results in a loss. An agent is only required to report written complaints to his employing principal, although it would be wise to report repeated oral complaints.

10. **D.** The use of information that has no basis in fact, such as a rumor, is prohibited.

11. **C.** Agents must always determine suitability before soliciting purchases or sales. The key here is that the agent recommended this stock to all clients. One investment cannot be suitable for the majority of your clients.

12. **D.** All of the practices are prohibited. An agent may not borrow money or securities from a customer unless that customer is a bank or broker/dealer in the business of lending money and/or securities. Selling speculative issues to a retired couple of modest means is an unsuitable transaction because it is not consistent with the objectives of the client. An agent must follow legal orders of the customer, even if the agent believes the order is an unwise one. An agent may not backdate confirmations (or any other records for that matter) for the benefit of the client.

13. **A.** An agent may indicate that a security is registered or is exempt from registration. All of the other statements are illegal.

14. **C.** Material facts are facts that an investor relies on to make investment decisions. The omission of a material fact in the sale, purchase, or offer of a security is fraudulent. This applies whether the security offered is exempt or nonexempt.

15. **B.** It can happen that a securities professional enters a personal order ahead of a client just by happenstance. There is no obligation to get the client the better price. Had the order been solicited, then we must be sure to place our customer's orders ahead of our own. Allowing a rumor to spread and then trading in response to it is a prohibited practice. Selling stock at the bid price and making up the difference with a personal check is a prohibited practice. Filling a firm's proprietary order ahead of a customer's order is a prohibited practice called front running.

16. **D.** Recommending tax shelters to low-income retirees is an example of an unsuitable transaction. Stating that an Administrator has approved an offering on the basis of the quality of information in the prospectus, soliciting retail orders for unregistered nonexempt securities, and employing a device to defraud are all prohibited practices under the USA.

17. **D.** As long as retaining custody of funds is not prohibited, an investment adviser may have custody of a customer's account after providing notice to the Administrator.

18. **A.** It is a prohibited practice under the USA for an agent to share in the profits or losses of a customer's account unless the customer and the employer have given written consent. Unlike FINRA rules, there is no requirement that the sharing be proportionate. Also, this type of sharing is only permitted for agents, not any of the other three securities professionals. An agent is permitted to jointly own a personal account at the firm and can refuse to share in a customer's account.

19. **D.** The rules regarding investment advisers and account trading are much more strict than those for broker/dealers because of the fiduciary responsibility of the adviser. Any action that results in a transaction in which the firm or an affiliate acts in either a principal or agency capacity requires written disclosure of that fact to the client and consent of the client prior to the completion of the trade.

20. **A.** Any change in the ownership of an investment advisory firm organized as a partnership, no matter how small, requires notification to all clients within a reasonable amount of time. If the firm is structured as a corporation, pledging a controlling interest in the company's stock is viewed as an assignment of the contracts. This may not be done without the approval of the clients. Agency cross transactions (i.e., transactions in which the adviser represents both sides of the trade) are permitted as long as the adviser makes the proper written disclosures and does not make buy/sell recommendations to either party.

21. **B.** Although Raymond is certainly in trouble and may have his registration revoked or suspended, the firm may also have problems. First, the Administrator may close the firm because of inadequate capital. It is also possible that the firm may face disciplinary action because of failure to properly supervise Raymond. Thirdly, the actions of a partner of a firm can lead to action against the firm. An agent cannot be an agent without representing a dealer, so this action would automatically terminate the licenses of all the agents who work for this firm.

22. **A.** It is illegal to intentionally omit a material fact that should have been disclosed to a customer. The definition includes the criterion of whether a reasonable person would attach decision-making importance to the omitted information to fully define the term *material fact*.

23. **B.** Nonpublic (inside) information of a material nature never may be used. All recommendations must be suitable, and recommendations are never approved by the Administrator.

24. **C.** It is appropriate to tell a customer that certain costs will be higher than normal, even if it is not known how much higher. In fact, it would be a prohibited practice to fail to inform the customer of such higher costs before the trade. All of the other choices are prohibited actions.

25. **C.** If the firm is a partnership, any change to a minority interest in that partnership requires notification to all clients within a reasonable period. Consent is required only before an assignment of the client's contract. All of the other choices meet the act's definition of *assignment*.

26. **B.** An investment adviser may not be compensated on the basis of capital gains in the client's account. Compensation may be based on a percentage rate of the average assets taken over a certain period.

27. **D.** All the answer choices involve fraudulent trading in response to insider information. Material information not available to the investing public cannot be used by anyone when making investment decisions.

28. **A.** You can never borrow money from a client who is not in the money lending business.

29. **C.** Opening a margin account is far more detailed than opening a cash account. There are a number of different agreements that have to be signed. The firm must obtain a properly executed written margin agreement promptly after the initial transaction in the account. The presence of an existing cash account is meaningless here.

30. **D.** NASAA rules permit bonuses to nonregistered personnel as long as the compensation is not directly tied to sales of securities.

QUICK QUIZ ANSWERS

Quick Quiz 4.A

1. **U.** It is unlawful to guarantee the performance of any security. Even though the government securities are guaranteed, the mutual fund investment is not.

2. **U.** It is unlawful to exercise discretion without prior written authorization. Because the client was a nondiscretionary client, the agent could not, on his own initiative, select which Internet company to invest in.

3. **L.** An agent must refuse orders from anyone other than the customer unless that person has prior written trading authority.

4. **U.** All written customer complaints must be forwarded to a designated supervisor of the agent's employing broker/dealer.

5. **L.** Agents may borrow from banks or financial institutions that are in the business of lending money to public customers. Agents may not borrow money from customers who are not in the business of lending money.

6. **U.** An agent may not guarantee the performance of a security.

7. **L.** It is lawful to charge extra transaction fees when justified as long as the customer is informed before the transaction.

8. **U.** It is unlawful to promise services that an agent cannot reasonably expect to perform or that the agent is not qualified to perform.

9. **U.** It is unlawful to solicit unregistered nonexempt securities.

Quick Quiz 4.B

1. **A.** Material disciplinary violations must be reported by all investment advisers, regardless of whether they keep custody. The first 2 answers fit the definition of material actions, but not the third. If the suit goes in favor of the client and the adviser is found guilty, disclosure would need to be made.

Quick Quiz 4.C

1. **C.** The USA does not require investment advisers to include in their contracts a list of states in which they are licensed to do business. The USA does require advisers to include their method of computing fees, a statement prohibiting assignment without client consent, and notification of change in membership of the investment partnership.

2. **F.** An Administrator may, by rule or order, prevent an adviser from taking custody. If an Administrator prevents custody, an adviser cannot overrule the Administrator by notifying the Administrator first.

3. **F.** An adviser may sell securities to clients from its own account provided disclosure is made as well as receipt of consent from the client before completion of the trade.

4. **T.** Investment advisers are bound by the regulations that apply to sales activities as well as those that apply to advisory activities. The reverse is also true. When a sales agent engages in investment advisory activities, the agent is bound by the rules that apply to providing investment advice to others as well as those that apply to sales practices.

Quick Quiz 4.D

1. **C.** Section 28(e) provides a safe harbor for those expenses paid with soft dollars that offer a direct research benefit. Rent is not included in the list of acceptable items coming under that safe harbor.

2. **D.** Soft-dollar compensation is when an investment adviser derives an economic benefit from the use of a client's commission dollars. Software of the type mentioned here is allowable under the safe harbor provisions of Section 28(e) of the Securities Exchange Act of 1934. It is true that this is indirect compensation and that this is a discretionary account, but the answer that best matches the question is soft dollar. Many times on the exam, you have to select best of the choices given.

Glossary

Numerics

12b-1 plan A section of the Investment Company Act of 1940 that permits an open-end investment company (mutual fund) to levy an ongoing charge for advertising and sales promotional expenses. This fee may not exceed .75% and, if above .25%, the fund may not describe itself as no-load.

A

accredited investor Any institution or individual meeting minimum requirements for the purchase of securities qualifying under the Regulation D registration exemption, as defined in Rule 501 of Regulation D.

An accredited investor generally is accepted to be one who:

- has a net worth, exclusive of the net equity in a primary residence, of $1 million or more; or

- has had an annual income of $200,000 or more in each of the two most recent years (or $300,000 jointly with a spouse) and who has a reasonable expectation of reaching the same income level in the current year.

administrator (1) The official or agency administering the securities laws of a state. (2) A person authorized by a court of law to liquidate the estate of an intestate decedent.

advertisement Any material designed for use by newspapers, magazines, radio, television, telephone recording, or any other public medium to solicit business. The firm using advertising has little control over the type of individuals being exposed to the advertising.

affiliate A person in a position to influence the policies of a corporation. This includes partners, officers, directors, and entities who control more than 10% of the voting stock.

agent (1) A securities salesperson who represents a broker/dealer or an issuer when selling or trying to sell securities to the investing public. This individual is considered an agent whether he actually receives or simply solicits orders. (2) A person acting for the accounts of others.

arbitrage The purchase of securities on one market and the simultaneous resale on another market to take advantage of a price discrepancy. This is not a form of market manipulation and is completely legal.

assessable stock Stock issued below par, carrying with it the option on the part of the issuer or creditors to assess the owner for the remainder. A gift of assessable stock is considered a sale under the Uniform Securities Act.

assignment Transferring an investment advisory contract to another firm. This may not be done without written consent of the customer. A change in the majority interest in an investment advisory firm organized as a partnership is also considered assignment.

associated person Any employee, manager, director, officer, or partner of a member broker/dealer or another entity (e.g., issuer, bank) or any person controlling, controlled by, or in common control with that member is considered an associated person of that member.

B

blue sky (v.) To qualify a securities offering in a particular state.

blue-sky laws The commonly used term for state regulations governing the securities industry.

bona fide From the Latin term for good faith. A bona fide offer is a sincere one.

breakpoint In the sale of mutual funds, the price points at which purchasers are entitled to a reduction in sales charge. One method of taking advantage of breakpoints is through the use of a letter of intent. *See* letter of intent, front-end load.

brochure rules An investment adviser must provide its customer with its brochure (Parts 2A and 2B of Form ADV) at least 48 hours before having him sign the contract. Failing that, the customer must be given five days to void the contract without penalty.

broker The role of a broker/dealer firm when it acts as an agent for a customer and charges the customer a commission for its services.

broker/dealer A firm that acts for the securities accounts of others (acting as a broker) or its own account (acting as a dealer) in trades. Excluded from the definition are:

- agents (registered representatives);

- issuers;

- banks, savings institutions, and trust companies; and

- firms that fit the definition, but (1) have no office in the state and (2) effect transactions only with accredited investors such as issuers, banks, insurance companies, or other broker/dealers, with nonresidents of the state, or with existing clients who have fewer than 30 days' residency in the state.

C

cancellation Nonpunitive termination of registration by the Administrator. Reasons include the registrant's death, its ceasing to do business, mental incompetence on the part of the registrant, or the Administrator's inability to locate the registrant.

cash account An account with a broker/dealer where securities purchases are paid for in full. *See* margin account.

CDSC Conditional deferred sales charge. Sometimes called a back-end load to differentiate between it and a front-end load. Instead of charging a load on each purchase, there is no sales charge unless the investor redeems shares too early. These charges begin reducing after the first year and generally decline to zero between the sixth and eighth year after purchase. *See* front-end load.

cease and desist A temporary, or summary, order the Administrator takes to prevent a securities violation. No prior notice or opportunity for a hearing is required for a summary action, but its provisions may not be enforced without a court order. The affected party may demand a hearing in writing, and the hearing must take place within 15 days of the Administrator's receipt of the written demand.

churning A prohibited practice in which a salesperson effects transactions in a customer's account that are excessive in size and/or frequency in relation to the size and character of the account.

commingling Mixing broker/dealer or investment adviser cash and securities with customer cash and securities in the same account. This is a prohibited practice.

commission A broker's fee for handling transactions for a client in an agency capacity.

consent to service of process A legal document entered into by all registrants, whereby the Administrator is given the power to accept legal papers on behalf of the registrant.

custody Maintaining possession of a customer's money and/or securities. Many states prohibit investment advisors from keeping custody. The others require the adviser to notify the Administrator if it intends to do so. An adviser is also considered to have custody if the customer has authorized it to receive and disperse funds and securities from his bank account.

D

dealer A firm acting as a principal, for its own account, in a trade. Such a firm actually owns the securities during the trade and charges its customer a markup (if the firm is selling the securities) or a markdown (if the firm is buying them).

discretion The authority for someone other than the beneficial owner of an account to make investment decisions for that account regarding the security, the number of shares or units, and whether to buy or sell. Decisions concerning only timing and price do not constitute discretion.

discretionary account An account in which the customer authorizes in writing a broker/dealer or investment adviser to use his judgment in buying and selling securities, including selection, timing, amount, and price. Judgment as to time and/or price only is not considered discretion. Discretionary trades must always be suitable for the customer.

E

effective date The date on which a security can be offered publicly if no stop order is submitted to the issuer by the Administrator.

electronic storage An acceptable method of recordkeeping, generally on computer disc. Among the requirements is that it cannot be altered and can be used to generate a paper copy upon request.

exempt security A security that need not be in formal compliance with a given piece of legislation, such as the Securities Act of 1933, or the Uniform Securities Act as adopted by a state. Examples are US government and municipal securities. No security is exempt from the antifraud provisions of any securities legislation.

exempt transaction A transaction exempt from registration, sales literature, and advertising requirements under the Uniform Securities Act. Examples of exempt transactions include:

- isolated nonissuer transactions;
- transactions with financial institutions (e.g., banks, savings institutions, trust companies, insurance companies, pension or profit-sharing plans, broker/dealers);
- unsolicited transactions;
- fiduciary transactions;
- private placement transactions;
- transactions between an issuer and its underwriters; and
- transactions with an issuer's employees, partners, or directors if no commission is paid directly or indirectly for the soliciting.

F

federal covered adviser An adviser regulated under the Investment Advisers Act of 1940. The person is either required to register with the SEC or is excluded from the definition of investment adviser under that act. A federal covered adviser has a federally imposed exemption from state securities regulation.

federal covered security A security with a federally imposed exemption from state registration. States not only need not register such securities; they are not allowed to. Examples are exchange-listed securities, investment company shares, and Nasdaq Stock Market securities.

fiduciary A person legally appointed and authorized to represent another person and act on that person's behalf.

foreign government securities Securities issued by the national government of a country with which the United States has diplomatic relations. Such securities are exempt from federal and state registration, but the foreign equivalent of municipal securities is nonexempt.

Form ADV The document used by an investment adviser to register with the appropriate authority. It consists of two basic parts, Part 1 and Part 2, with each of those divided into two parts, 1A and 1B and 2A and 2B. The Part 1 is used to disclose information to the regulators and the Part 2 is used to meet the brochure requirements for disclosures to clients.

fraud The deliberate concealment, misrepresentation, or omission of material information or the truth to deceive or manipulate another party for unlawful or unfair gain.

front-end load When discussing the sale of mutual fund shares, the amount of sales charge levied on each purchase. The maximum permitted load is 8.5% of the offering price, but most funds today charge 5% or less. This load can be reduced by reaching a breakpoint. *See* breakpoint, letter of intent, CDSC.

front running Taking action to profit from a customer order before executing the order. Example: if the customer places a large order for a particular stock, the agent might purchase calls on the stock before placing the order and then profit from any price rise caused by the order. This is a prohibited practice.

G

government security An obligation of the US government, backed by the full faith and credit of the government, and regarded as the highest grade or safest issue (i.e., default risk free). The US government issues short-term Treasury bills, medium-term Treasury notes, and long-term Treasury bonds.

guaranteed Securities that have a guarantee, usually from a source other than the issuer, as to the payment of principal, interest, or dividends.

H

hypothecation When securities are purchased in a margin account, they are pledged as collateral for the loan made by the broker/dealer to the client. When these securities are pledged, they are said to be hypothecated. Clients must sign a written hypothecation agreement promptly after the initial margin transaction in their account. *See* margin account.

I

inside information Material and nonpublic information a person obtained or used for the purpose of trading in securities. *See also* material fact.

insider Any person who has nonpublic knowledge (material information) about a corporation. Insiders include directors, officers, and stockholders who own more than 10% of any class of equity security of a corporation.

institutional account An account held for the benefit of others. Examples include banks, trusts, pension and profit-sharing plans, mutual funds, and insurance companies.

institutional investor Institutional investors are covered by fewer protective regulations because it is assumed that they are more knowledgeable and better able to protect themselves. The Uniform Securities Act includes in its definition of institutional clients: a bank, savings institution, trust company, insurance company, investment company, as defined in the Investment Company Act of 1940, or employee benefit plan with assets of not less than one million dollars ($1,000,000).

investment adviser Any person who, for compensation (a flat fee or a percentage of assets managed), is in the business of offering investment advice on securities.

investment adviser representative Any partner, officer, director, or other individual employed by or associated with an investment adviser who (1) gives investment advice or makes recommendations; (2) manages client accounts or portfolios; (3) determines which investment recommendations or advice should be given; (4) offers or sells investment advisory services; or (5) supervises employees involved in any of these activities.

Investment Advisers Act of 1940 Legislation passed by Congress that requires certain investment advisers to register as such with the SEC, to abide by the Investment Advisers Act of 1940 and all other applicable federal acts, and to treat its customers in a fair and equitable manner.

investment company A company engaged primarily in the business of investing and trading in securities, including face-amount certificate companies, unit investment trusts, and management companies.

Investment Company Act of 1940 Congressional legislation enacted to regulate investment companies that requires any investment company in interstate commerce to register with the SEC.

isolated nonissuer transaction An exempt transaction between individual investors, conducted privately. The exempt nature of the transaction must be established by a principal for each separate trade.

issuer (1) The corporation, government, or other entitiy that offers its securities for sale. (2) According to the USA, any person who issues or proposes to issue any security. When a corporation or municipality raises additional capital through an offering of securities, that corporation or municipality is the issuer of those securities.

L

letter of intent A non-binding agreement between a purchaser of mutual funds and the fund underwriter that allows the investor up to 13 months to reach a specified dollar purchase. In so doing, the client receives the sales charge reduction applicable to that breakpoint with the first and subsequent purchases. *See* breakpoint, front-end load.

M

margin The use of borrowed money to purchase securities.

margin account An account with a broker/dealer where the firm lends 50% of the purchase price to the client with the client putting up the balance. Such accounts use leverage and carry greater risk than cash accounts. *See* cash account, hypothecation.

markdown The profit made by a dealer when purchasing a security from a customer. *See* markup.

market maker A dealer willing to accept the risk of holding securities to facilitate trading in a particular security(ies).

markup The profit made by a dealer when selling a security to a customer. Just as in any business, dealers purchase at one price and sell to their clients at a higher one. That difference is the markup. *See* markdown.

matched orders Simultaneously buying and selling a security to give its trading volume a falsely high appearance. This is a prohibited practice.

material fact Information required to be included in a registration statement that a knowledgeable investor would deem significant in making an investment determination. *See also* inside information.

municipal security Exempt debt security issued by some level of government other than the federal to raise money for a public project. Interest payable on these instruments is not federally taxable.

N

National Conference of Commissioners on Uniform State Laws (NCCUSL) The NCCUSL, founded in 1892, is an organization composed of lawyers who draft and propose template state legislation where uniformity in law among the states is deemed to be desirable. It was the NCCUSL that wrote the Uniform Securities Act. The organization does not, of course, actually write laws, but rather proposes legislation that a state may adopt if it chooses.

National Securities Markets Improvement Act of 1996 (NSMIA) Federal legislation designed to clarify the demarcation between federal and state securities law and to improve the efficiency of the securities markets in the United States. Some securities, known as federal covered securities, and some advisory firms, known as federal covered advisers, were removed from state purview to eliminate duplication of regulatory effort.

no load The term used to describe a mutual fund whose shares are offered without any sales charge. The term may not be used if the fund has a 12b-1 plan with a charge in excess of .25%.

nonexempt security A security whose issue and sale must be in compliance with the Uniform Securities Act and/or the various federal securities acts. Most corporate securities are nonexempt.

nonissuer A person other than the issuer of a security. In a nonissuer securities transaction, for example, the issuer is not one of the parties in the transaction, and the transaction, therefore, is not, according to the law, directly or indirectly for the benefit of the issuer. When the USA refers to a nonissuer transaction, it is referring to a transaction in which the proceeds of the sale go to the selling stockholder. Most nonissuer transactions also are called secondary transactions.

North American Securities Administrators Association (NASAA) The NASAA, founded in Kansas in 1919, is the oldest international investor protection organization. Its current membership is 67 Administrators from the territories, districts, and states of the United States, from Mexico, and from the provinces of Canada. The Series 63 is written by the NASAA and administered by FINRA.

notice filing Procedure under the Uniform Securities Act whereby an issuer notifies state securities administrators of federal registration.

NSMIA See National Securities Markets Improvement Act of 1996.

O

offer (1) Under the USA, every attempt to solicit a purchase or sale in a security for value. (2) An indication by an investor, trader, or dealer of a willingness to sell a security or commodity.

oversubscribed The term used to describe a new security issue where the demand for the shares greatly exceeds the available supply. These issues usually appreciate rapidly on the first day of trading and failure to properly allocate them is a prohibited practice.

P

painting the Tape Spurious trading in a particular security among a group of collaborating investors to give a falsely high appearance of interest in the security. This is a prohibited practice.

person In general, any entity that can be held to a contract: an individual, corporation, trust, government, political subdivision, and unincorporated association are examples.

preorganization certificate Agreement for the future purchase of the stock of a corporation when it is eventually formed. Distribution of preorganization certificates is an exempt transaction, provided certain conditions are met.

private placement The USA's private placement provision allows an exemption from full state registration for a security that is offered in that state to no more than 10 noninstitutional investors within a 12-month period.

prospectus The legal document that must be given to every investor who purchases registered securities in an offering. It describes the details of the company and the particular offering.

Q

quotation The price given for a security. It consists of two numbers, the bid and the ask or offer. The bid price is what the dealer is willing to pay a customer who is selling the security and the ask is the selling price by a dealer to a customer who is buying. *Syn* quote.

R

registered investment company An investment company, such as an open-end management company (mutual fund) or closed-end management company, that is registered with the SEC and exempt from state registration and regulation.

registration by coordination A security is eligible for blue-sky registration by coordination in a state if the issuer files for registration of that security under the Securities Act of 1933 and files duplicates of the registration documents with the state Administrator. The state registration becomes effective at the same time the federal registration statement becomes effective.

registration by qualification A security is eligible for blue-sky registration by qualification in a state if all of the offering is to be sold in a single state or if the security is not eligible for another method of state registration. Net worth and disclosure requirements apply, and registration does not become effective until the Administrator so orders.

registration statement Before nonexempt securities can be offered to the public, they require registration under the Securities Act of 1933 and/or the Uniform Securities Act. The registration statement must disclose all pertinent information concerning the issuer and the offering. This statement is submitted to the SEC and/or Administrator in accordance with the requirements of their respective laws. If the securities are to be sold in only a single state, by qualification, only that state's registration requirements apply.

rescission Buying back, from the customer, a security that was inadvertently sold unlawfully. The price is generally the customer's purchase price plus the state's legal rate of interest less any income received. The customer has 30 days to accept or reject the offer.

S

Securities Act of 1933 The federal legislation requiring the full and fair disclosure of all material information about the issuance of new securities.

Securities and Exchange Commission (SEC) The commission Congress created to protect investors, which enforces the Securities Act of 1933, the Securities Exchange Act of 1934, the Investment Company Act of 1940, the Investment Advisers Act of 1940, and other securities laws.

Securities Exchange Act of 1934 The federal legislation establishing the Securities and Exchange Commission that regulates securities exchanges and over-the-counter markets and protects investors from unfair and inequitable practices.

security An investment instrument represented by a certificate or other securitized document, ownership of which yields unpredictable profits or losses that stem from the actions of a third party, usually the issuer of the security. Examples are stocks, bonds, notes, certificates of interest in investment or marketing plans, and options on commodities or on other securities. Whole life insurance, with its table of guaranteed cash values, is not a security, but variable life is. A fixed annuity, with its guaranteed monthly payout, is not a security, but a variable annuity is. A futures contract, with its set terms, is not a security, but an option on that contract is.

self-regulatory organization (SRO) An entity that is accountable to the SEC for the enforcement of federal securities laws, as well as for the supervision of securities practices, within an assigned field of jurisdiction. Examples are FINRA, the various stock exchanges, the Municipal Securities Rulemaking Board, and the Chicago Board Options Exchange.

sell The act of conveying ownership of a security or other property for money or other value; every contract to sell a security or an interest in a security. Sales include the following.

- Any security given or delivered with, or as a bonus for, any purchase of securities is considered to have been offered and sold for value.

- A gift of assessable stock is considered to involve an offer and sale.

- Every sale or offer of a warrant or right to purchase or subscribe to another security is considered to include an offer of the other security.

  Sales do not include bona fide pledges or loans or stock dividends if nothing of value is given by the stockholders for the dividend.

solicited order An order resulting from a broker/dealer recommendation. The resulting trade must be suitable for the investor.

stop order Action the Administrator takes to prevent a registration of a security in his state. Unlike cease and desist orders, stop orders require prior notice to the affected party and a hearing with a written finding.

suitable transaction A transaction that meets or takes into account the investment needs of the customer. All solicited transactions must be suitable.

surety bond A bond required for many employees, officers, and partners of broker/dealers and investment advisers to protect clients against acts of misplacement, fraudulent trading, and check forgery.

T

testimonial A statement in an advertisement or other promotional release, usually by a client, indicating great satisfaction with the provider of goods or services. Testimonials may never be used by investment advisers or their representatives.

transfer agent A person or an organization responsible for recording the names of registered stockholders and the number of shares owned, seeing that the certificates are signed by the appropriate corporate officers, affixing the corporate seal, and delivering the securities to the transferee.

U

underwriter The entity responsible for marketing stocks, bonds, mutual fund shares, and so forth.

Uniform Securities Act (USA) Template legislation written by the NCCUSL to serve as the basis for a state's securities legislation if it wished to adopt it. It regulates securities, persons (broker/dealers and their agents and investment advisers and their representatives), and transactions in the securities markets within the state. All but a few of the states have adopted the USA in some form.

unsolicited order An order originated by the customer, not the result of a broker/dealer recommendation. The resulting trade is an exempt transaction, though written customer acknowledgment of its unsolicited nature may be required by the Administrator.

unsuitable transaction A transaction that does not meet the investment needs of the customer. An example is purchase of a municipal bond for a low-income customer seeking growth.

W

withdrawal Voluntary termination of registration on the part of the registrant, through submission of Form ADV-W. Withdrawal is effective within 30 days under the Uniform Securities Act unless the Administrator makes a contrary finding.

wrap account An investment advisory account in which all management fees and commissions are combined and paid, usually quarterly, as a percentage of assets under management.

Index

A

accredited investor 64
administrative personnel, exclusions from definition of agent 14
administrator
  cease and desist orders 83
  investigations and subpoenas 83
  judicial review of orders (appeal) 94
  jurisdiction and powers 77–78
  making, amending, rescinding rules and orders 83–84
  registration denial, suspension, cancellation, or revocation 86–89
agency cross transaction 128
agents
  definition and exclusions 14–15
  fee and commission sharing 17
  financial requirements 16
  jurisdiction of state law 8
  registration requirements 16–17
arbitrage 114
assessable stock 80
assignment of advisory contract 131

B

bankruptcy, guardian, or conservator transactions 62
banks, broker/dealer subsidiaries of 9
blue-sky laws 4
breakpoints 117
broker/dealers
  defined 9
  denial, suspension, cancellation, or revocation of registration 86–87
  exclusions from definition 9–11
  financial requirements 12
  jurisdiction of state law 8
  no place of business in the state exclusion 10
  post-registration requirements 36
  registration requirements 11–12, 26–28

C

cancellation, of registration 88
cease and desist orders, issued by Administrator 83
change of residence 10
churning 110
civil liabilities, under Uniform Securities Act 90–91
compensation 20
complaints 116
consent to service of process 34
contingent deferred sales load (CDSC) 117
contumacy 84
coordination, registration by 56
criminal penalties, for violations of Uniform Securities Act 90–91
CTRs. *See* Currency Transaction Reports
Currency Transaction Reports 143

D

depository institutions 60
discretion 111

E

effective date (of registration) 58
email retention requirements 37
employee benefit plans, securities issued by 61
escrow 68

F

federal covered securities 53–54
federally covered investment companies
  notice filing for 56
fiduciary responsibilities 127
  investment advisory contracts 127–128
  investment advisory fees 130
Financial Modernization Act (1999) 9
financial planners 19
foreign government securities 60

G

government securities 60
Gramm-Leach-Bliley Act (1999) 9

H

hearings 85
Howey Decision 51
hypothecation 113

I

initial public offering (IPO) 53
injunctions 83
institutional investor 63
institutional investor transactions 63
insurance company securities 61
investigations, conducted by Administrator 83
investment advice
  fiduciary responsibilities 127
  fraudulent and prohibited practices 121–128
  rights of recovery from improper 91
investment adviser representatives 34–36
  defined 28
  denial, suspension, cancellation, or revocation of registration 86–87
  exclusions from definition 32
investment advisers
  defined 18–20
  denial, suspension, cancellation, or revocation of registration 86–87
  exclusions from definition 21–22
  exemption from registration 24
  federal covered 22–24
  financial requirements 28–30

F

fraud 93
fraudulent and prohibited practices (providing investment advice) 121–124
front running 114, 116

net worth requirements 28
  registration 26
investment advisory contracts 115,
  127–128
investment advisory fees 129, 130
investment company securities 55
investments, nonsecurity versus
  security 52
isolated nonissuer transactions 62
issuers 53
  personnel representing, excluded
    from definition of agent 14–15
issuer transactions 53

L

lack of qualification as reason for
  denial of registration 86
legal jurisdiction 80, 152
  publishing and broadcast
    exceptions to 81–82
letter of rescission 91
limited offering transactions 63

M

matched orders 114
ministerial employees 14
municipal securities 60

N

National Conference of
  Commissioners on Uniform State
  Laws (NCCUSL) 3
National Securities Markets
  Improvement Act (NSMIA) 1,
  55–56
net capital requirements, for broker/
  dealers 12
net worth requirements, for
  investment advisers 28
non-assessable stock 80
nonexempt security 53
nonissuer transactions 53
nonprofit organizations, securities
  issued by 61
North American Securities
  Administrators Association
  (NASAA) 3
notice filing 23
notification (filing) 56
  qualifications 56–57

O

offer (offer to sell) 106
ongoing reports 67
order ticket 108
OTC Bulletin Board 57

P

pension consultants 20
Pink Sheets 57
pledgees, nonissuer transactions by
  64
power of attorney 111
pre-organization certificates 63
primary public offering. *See* initial
  public offering (IPO)
primary transaction. *See* issuer
  transaction
private placement 63
prospectus delivery requirements 68
public utility securities 61
publishing and broadcast exceptions
  to jurisdiction 81–82

Q

qualification, registration by 58

R

registrant 8
registration of securities 55–60
  by coordination 56
  by qualification 58
  denial, suspension, cancellation,
    or revocation of 86–87
  notice filing 56
  ongoing reports 67
  withdrawal of statement 67
Regulation D private placements 55
right of rescission 91–92
Rule 12b-1 117

S

safe harbor
  Section 28(e) Soft Dollars 138
sale (sell) 152
sales of securities at financial
  institutions 142
SEC Release IA-1092 19
Section 28(e) of the Securities
  Exchange Act of 1934 138
securities. *See also* registration

excluded items 52
exempt 54
federal covered 53–54
fraudulent sale of 90
Howey Decision 51
included items 52–53
nonexempt 53
offer or offer to sell 106
rights of recovery from improper
  sale 91–92
state registration of 56–60
Securities Investors Protection
  Corporation (SIPC) coverage 143
securities professional, denial,
  suspension, cancellation, or
  revocation of registration 86–89
Self Regulatory Organization (SRO)
  7
selling away 119
snowbirds 10
soft-dollar arrangements 138
soft-dollar compensation 139
solicitor 7
splitting commissions 120
sports and entertainment
  representatives 19
statue of limitations
  for civil provisions 90
  for criminal penalties 93
stop order 4, 85, 87
subpoenas, issued by Administrator
  83
successor firm 35
summarily 4
summary order 4
surety bonds 12–13, 28, 137

T

trading authorization 111
transactions
  bankruptcy, guardian, or
    conservator 62
  institutional investor 63
  limited offering 63
  underwriter 59
  unit secured 64
  with existing security holders 64

U

underwriter transactions 62
Uniform Securities Act (USA) 1.
  See also registration
  agents 13–17

bonding 12, 28, 137
broker/dealers 9–13
civil liabilities 90–91
consent to service of process 34
criminal penalties 90–91
filing fees 35, 67
financial reports and
  recordkeeping requirements 36
fraudulent and prohibited
  practices in sale of securities 53
fraudulent and prohibited
  practices when providing
  investment advice 121–129
general registration procedures
  34–37

investment adviser representatives
  26–28
investment advisers 18–25
issuer 53
judicial review of orders (appeal)
  94
sale or sell and offer or offer to sell
  106
securities (inclusions and
  exclusions) 49–50
state registration 56
United Sates government securities
  60
unsolicited brokerage transactions 62
using the Internet 141

V

vacated 87

W

waivers 117
wash trades 114
withdrawal of registration 88–89
wrap fee programs 29

Notes

Notes

Notes

Notes

Notes

Notes

Notes

Notes

Notes

Notes

Notes

Notes

Notes

Notes

Notes